Hegel's Epistemology

Hegel's Epistemology

A Philosophical Introduction to the *Phenomenology of Spirit*

Kenneth R. Westphal

Hackett Publishing Company, Inc.
Indianapolis/Cambridge

Copyright © 2003 by Hackett Publishing Company, Inc.

All rights reserved
Printed in the United States of America

09 08 07 06 05 04 03   1 2 3 4 5 6 7

For further information, please address:

Hackett Publishing Company, Inc.
P.O. Box 44937
Indianapolis, IN 46244-0937

www.hackettpublishing.com

Cover design by Abigail Coyle
Text design by Meera Dash
Composition by Agnew's, Inc.
Printed at Sheridan Books, Inc.

Library of Congress Cataloging-in-Publication Data

Westphal, Kenneth R.
    Hegel's epistemology : a philosophical introduction to the Phenomenology of spirit / Kenneth R. Westphal.
       p.   cm.
    Includes bibliographical references and indexes.
    ISBN 0-87220-646-7 (cloth) — ISBN 0-87220-645-9 (pbk.)
    1. Hegel, Georg Wilhelm Friedrich, 1770–1831. Phènomenologie des Geistes. 2. Knowledge, Theory of. I. Title.

B2929.W465   2003
193—dc21

                                                                                 2003044997

The paper used in this publication meets the minimum requirements on American National Standard for Information Sciences—Permanence of Paper for Printed Library Materials, ANSIZ39.48-1984.

Contents

	Analytical Table of Contents	vii
	Acknowledgments	xi
	References and Abbreviations	xv
ONE	Introduction	1
TWO	Introducing Hegel's Phenomenological Method	7
THREE	Internal Critique in Sophocles' *Antigone*	14
FOUR	Philosophical Reflection and Philosophical Method	29
FIVE	The Basic Features of Hegel's Solution to the Dilemma of the Criterion	38
SIX	Some Key Points of Hegel's Epistemology	51
SEVEN	Some Contemporary Points of Relevance of Hegel's Epistemology	72
EIGHT	Hegel and Twentieth-Century Empiricism	82
NINE	Information Theory and Social Epistemology	92
TEN	Methodological Individualism, Moderate Collectivism, and Social Epistemology	103
	Recommended Readings	117
	Bibliography	125
	Name Index	137
	Subject Index	139

Analytical Table of Contents

	Acknowledgments	xi
	References and Abbreviations	xv
ONE	INTRODUCTION	1
TWO	INTRODUCING HEGEL'S PHENOMENOLOGICAL METHOD	7
THREE	INTERNAL CRITIQUE IN SOPHOCLES' *ANTIGONE*	14
	3 A Literary Model of Hegel's Philosophical Method	14
	4 Creon as a Form of Consciousness	14
	5 The Internal Critique of Creon's Form of Consciousness in *Antigone*	17
	6 Summary of the Internal Critique of Creon in *Antigone*	26
FOUR	PHILOSOPHICAL REFLECTION AND PHILOSOPHICAL METHOD	29
	7 Reflections on Judgment and Reflective Judgment in *Antigone*	29
	8 Reflective Judgment in Hegel's Phenomenological Method	34
FIVE	THE BASIC FEATURES OF HEGEL'S SOLUTION TO THE DILEMMA OF THE CRITERION	38
	9 Rational Justification and the Dilemma of the Criterion	38
	10 Hegel's Analysis of the Self-Critical Structure of Consciousness	40
	11 Mature Judgment, Fallibilism, and Pragmatic Rationality	47

	SIX	SOME KEY POINTS OF HEGEL'S EPISTEMOLOGY	51
		12 Key Theses of Hegel's Epistemology	51
		13 Hegel's Key Epistemological Arguments in the *Phenomenology*	56
		14 Chart of the Structure of Hegel's Epistemological Argument in the *Phenomenology of Spirit*	65
		15 Summary of Hegel's Transcendental Argument for Realism	65
	SEVEN	SOME CONTEMPORARY POINTS OF RELEVANCE OF HEGEL'S EPISTEMOLOGY	72
		16 Realism and the Social and Historical Aspects of Human Knowledge	72
		17 Cognitive Activity and Realism about the Objects of Human Knowledge	72
		18 Justificatory "Coherence" and Realism about the Objects of Human Knowledge	73
		19 Hegel's Semantic Externalism	75
		20 Reason versus Tradition?	77
	EIGHT	HEGEL AND TWENTIETH-CENTURY EMPIRICISM	82
		21 Hegel's Justification of (Pure) A Priori Conceptions	82
		22 Perceptual Synthesis and the Identification of Objects	85
		23 The Significance of Rejecting Reductionism	87
		24 Philosophy, History, and History of Philosophy	89
	NINE	INFORMATION THEORY AND SOCIAL EPISTEMOLOGY	92
		25 Justification through Internal Critique	92
		26 Key Features of Dretske's Information-Theoretic Epistemology	93

	27	Information Channels and Human Knowledge	94
	28	Internalism and Externalism in Hegel's Epistemology	98
TEN		METHODOLOGICAL INDIVIDUALISM, MODERATE COLLECTIVISM, AND SOCIAL EPISTEMOLOGY	103
	29	Individualism in Recent Epistemology	103
	30	Some Basic Problems with Individualism in Epistemology	104
	31	Some Individualist Rejoinders	105
	32	Individualism, Holism, and Hegel's Moderate Collectivism	107
	33	Substantive Individualism in Recent Epistemology	109
	34	Holism and Hegel's Moderate Collectivism	110
	35	Moderate Collectivism and "the" Subject of Knowledge	112
	36	Hegel's Moderate Collectivism versus "Plural Subjects"	113
	37	The Barrenness of the "Individualism–Holism" Dispute	114

Recommended Readings	117
Bibliography	125
Name Index	137
Subject Index	139

Acknowledgments

I began studying Hegel's epistemology as an undergraduate when, scandalized by Kuhn's apparent attack on realism in the philosophy of science and appalled by the simple-minded relativism so widely espoused in popular culture, I became convinced by Richard Schacht, perhaps unwittingly, that if anyone had thought through relativism from the inside out and won, it was Hegel. My sense that Hegel's "idealism" is in fact a realist form of holism took longer to work out. I remain deeply grateful to Michael Theunissen, with whom I studied in Berlin, for confirming my interpretation of Hegel's ontology.

Graduate studies at the University of Wisconsin-Madison provided me with repeated and intensive training in philosophizing historically. I was inspired by the outstanding caliber of scholarship in ancient philosophy, such as Akrill, Owen, Owens, and Vlastos. Those scholars, along with the great Kant commentaries by Vaihinger, Paton, Kemp Smith, and de Vleeshauer, and Kemp Smith's monumental works on Descartes and especially Hume, formed my model of rigorous, historically based philosophy.

My training in analytic epistemology began as an undergraduate at the University of Illinois, Urbana-Champaign with Bill Alston, who drew my attention, inter alia, to Dretske's *Seeing and Knowing*. In graduate school my training in epistemology and philosophy of science continued with Fred Dretske. It has been both an honor and an incalculable benefit to have had the tuition of these two past masters of their craft. To them I dedicate this heretical little book. I hope they will not be too chagrined by what has become of one of their most avid students.

I mention these points about my background in order to suggest that, when these kinds of philosophical and interpretive resources are brought to bear on Hegel's philosophy, they reveal a surprisingly different content and character of Hegel's actual views. These resources reveal that Hegel was, among much else, an acute epistemologist with many abiding insights. That these are actually Hegel's views is best shown by the convergence of three crucial standards of interpretive adequacy: to provide a complete philosophical reconstruction of an historical text, to do this within its historical and philosophical context, and to provide good philosophical sense for both the structure and the details of that text, down to individual lines, phrases, and terms. Obviously, these standards can only be approximated by parts of the present synopsis of Hegel's epistemology. In other research that underwrites this synopsis, I have sought to fulfill these requirements conjointly and believe I have done so, certainly to a degree uncommon in Hegel studies. For enabling me to acquire, use, and develop these abilities, I remain indebted, deeply and gratefully, to my teachers.

This book began with an article on the contemporary relevance of Hegel's epistemology delivered to the Hegel Society of Great Britain and published in their *Bulletin*, "Is Hegel's *Phenomenology* Relevant to Contemporary Epistemology?" (Westphal 2000c). I thank the Society for inviting me to compose my thoughts on these issues. I thank Bob Scharff for suggesting that I develop this article into the short book it has become, and I thank Jeff Edwards and Don Welton for seconding Bob's suggestion so resoundingly. This book was completed by composing Chapters 2 through 4. I am very grateful to Linda Napolitano Valditara for her invitation to crystallize my thoughts on these issues and for her incisive comments on my penultimate draft of this material.

I wish finally to thank those at Hackett Publishing, especially Deborah Wilkes, for their keen interest in this project, for obtaining excellent reader's reports, and for their expert preparation and production of my text. Final preparations of the text were completed while on study leave provided by the Arts and Humanities Research Board (AHRB, UK), whom I thank for their support. My last and very special thanks go to two anonymous readers, whose acute comments and constructive suggestions contributed significantly to what follows. I regret that I can only indirectly attribute this most direct of philosophical debts.

TÜBINGEN
1 OCTOBER 2002

* * *

Material appearing in Chapters 2 through 4 originally appeared in Italian under the title, "L'ispirazione tragica della dialettica fenomenologica di Hegel," in Linda Napolitano Valditara, ed., *Antichi e nuovi dialoghi di sapienti ed eroi* (Trieste: Edizioni Università di Trieste, 2002), 151–77.

Material appearing in §12 is drawn from my entry, "Hegel," in Ernest Sosa and Jonathan Dancy, eds., *A Companion to Epistemology* (Oxford: Blackwell, 1992), 167–70.

Material appearing in §13 and in Chapters 7 through 10 is based on my article, "Is Hegel's *Phenomenology* Relevant to Contemporary Epistemology?" *Bulletin of the Hegel Society of Great Britain* 41/42 (2000): 43–85.

The chart in §14 is drawn from *Hegel's Epistemological Realism: A Study of the Aim and Method of Hegel's Phenomenology of Spirit* (Dordrecht and Boston: Kluwer, 1989), 156–7.

§15 is drawn from my article, "Can Pragmatic Realists Argue Transcendentally?" in John Shook, ed., *Pragmatic Naturalism and Realism* (Buffalo, N.Y.: Prometheus, 2003), 151–75.

I gratefully thank the editors and presses in which these materials originally appeared for their kind permission to reuse them here. All of them have been variously revised for this book.

References and Abbreviations

I have used the author, date, and page method of citation almost exclusively. The full reference for materials cited in this way are found in the Bibliography under the author and date cited.

In a few cases it is more effective to use the following abbreviations. Multivolume works are cited by volume and page number thus: *CP* 6:52. Occasionally, "ch." designates chapters.

PhdG Hegel, *Phänomenologie des Geistes* (Hegel 1980; *GW* 9).

GW Hegel, *Gesammelte Werke* (Hegel 1968–).

M Miller, tr., *Hegel's Phenomenology of Spirit* (Hegel 1977). Hegel's *Phenomenology* is cited by the initials of its German title, including (when necessary) page and line references to the critical edition of the *Phänomenologie des Geistes* (*GW* 9). Page references to Miller's translation follow after a slash thus: (*PhdG* 9:58.13–4/M52).

Enz. Hegel, *Encyclopedia of Philosophical Sciences* (Hegel 1831). This three-volume work contains Hegel's shorter *Logic, Philosophy of Nature,* and *Philosophy of Spirit.* It is divided into consecutively numbered sections that are cited thus: *Enz.* §98.

Rph Hegel, *Elements of the Philosophy of Right* (Hegel 1991). This work, too, is divided into consecutively numbered sections, referred to thus: *Rph* §135. Occasionally, Hegel's own published remarks are indicated by an "R" suffix to a section number; notes on Hegel's lectures supplied by his editors are indicated with a "Z" (*Zusatz*) suffix.

KdrV Kant, *Critique of Pure Reason.* Kant's *Critique of Pure Reason* appeared in two significantly different editions. The standard convention is to refer to the first edition as "A" and the second as "B." Since this method of citation is unique in the field, in most cases I simply refer to "A" and "B" page references (e.g., A182–4/B225–7) without including *KdrV.* The original pagination of the two German editions is carried through all recent translations of Kant's first *Critique.*

PH Sextus Empiricus, *Outlines of Pyrrhonism* (Sextus Empiricus 1934). This work is contained in the first of the four volumes of Sextus Empiricus' *Works* (1934). The abbreviation derives from the Latin title, *Pyrrhoniae Hypotyposes*. This work is cited by book and section numbers thus: *PH* I §§112–4. Very occasionally, other works by Sextus are cited by volume, book, and section numbers thus: 2:IV §§15–8.

CP Russell, *The Collected Papers of Bertrand Russell* (Russell 1994). Russell's collected papers are cited by volume and page numbers thus: *CP* 9:45.

KFI Dretske, *Knowledge and the Flow of Information* (Dretske 1981).

ONE

Introduction

1 Hegel's *Phenomenology* is notoriously challenging, in form and structure as well as in content. His apparent ambitions in the *Phenomenology* and his highly unusual presentation have often made it difficult to relate it to more familiar philosophical views and issues. Hegel demands much of his readers. At the beginning of a chapter or subsection, for example, Hegel states a philosophical view often to argue (by indirect proof or reductio ad absurdum) against that view, though sometimes only to argue against a defective account or justification of that view. Precisely what view he criticizes can at times be difficult to determine, often because he states some essential points of an historical philosopher's view without mentioning whose view it is. Hegel unfortunately tends to refer to passages from the history of philosophy the way Medieval philosophers referred to Aristotle. They would write "the philosopher says . . . ," expecting, and knowing they could expect, the reader to know exactly which passage from which work of Aristotle's was being quoted or paraphrased. Hegel, however, only rarely mentions his frequent paraphrasing or quotation—though his use of such references should not have misfired nearly so often as it has.

Three examples illustrate these points nicely. Russell famously complains that Hegel fails to distinguish "the 'is' of identity" from "the 'is' of predication."[1] However, Russell didn't recognize that Hegel conflated them only as an assumed first premise of a reductio ad absurdum argument to show that identity is distinct from predication![2] A second example comes from the critical German edition of Hegel's works, which has performed an enormous service in tracking down a plethora of possible and definite references or allusions that Hegel makes to other philosophers. However, Hegel's second chapter, "Perception," defied those efforts; the critical apparatus contains only eight references for it, all of them merely cross-references within Hegel's text (*GW* 9:495). In fact, "Perception" is all about Hume's epistemology in the *Treatise of Human Nature*, specifically, in "Of Scepticism with regard to the senses" (I.iv §2).[3]

---

1. Russell (1914), 48–9 note; *CP* 6:365.
2. Westphal (1998a), §7.
3. Ibid., passim.

A third example is especially important for the present discussion: in the middle of the Introduction to the *Phenomenology,* Hegel paraphrases exactly the Dilemma of the Criterion from Sextus Empiricus' *Outlines of Pyrrhonism.*[4] Roderick Chisholm (1973, 1) called this Dilemma "one of the most important and one of the most difficult of all the problems of philosophy."[5] It has received only scant attention from analytic epistemologists, and far less from Hegel scholars. Yet the Dilemma of the Criterion is the central methodological issue of the *Phenomenology of Spirit,* to which Hegel provides by far the most sophisticated and successful response I have found anywhere.

Thus one reason why it is so fitting to introduce Hegel's *Phenomenology of Spirit* in view of his epistemology is that epistemology is central to the *Phenomenology,* it is central to philosophy, and it is central to much philosophical education. Introducing Hegel's *Phenomenology* via his epistemology is also timely because philosophers are once again occupied with issues that occupied Hegel: conflicts between realism and historicist relativism. Generally, realism is conjoined with individualist theories of knowledge, while historicist relativism is associated with social or nonindividualist theories of knowledge. One key aim of Hegel's *Phenomenology* is to show that a properly constructed social and historical theory of human knowledge requires realism about the objects of our knowledge. By the same token, one reason Hegel's epistemology has gone unrecognized is that philosophers have too often supposed that combining realism with a social and historical epistemology is impossible. "Realism," as used here, is the view that things (of whatever sort) exist and have characteristics unto themselves (e.g., our bodies and the rest of the natural world), regardless of what we think, say, or believe about them. "Epistemological realism," then, specifies further that we can know at least something about such things.[6]

---

4. Westphal (1989a), 11, 14; (1998b); and Chapter 5 in this book.

5. He immediately adds: "I am tempted to say that one has not begun to philosophise until one has faced this problem and has recognized how unappealing, in the end, each of the possible solutions is" (1). Unfortunately, Chisholm unduly restricted his list of possible solutions by ignoring the possibility and prospects of self-criticism.

6. When introducing technical terms in this discussion, such as those just used, I have tried to characterize them briefly, clearly, and adequately for present purposes. Further discussion of these terms and their associated issues may be found in the Blackwell *Companion to Epistemology* or in the *Routledge Encyclopedia of Philosophy.*

SECTION 1   3

To say that Hegel's *Phenomenology* is centrally epistemological immediately poses another problem: it certainly doesn't *read* like epistemology in any familiar sense. Hegel's *Phenomenology* has a complex expository structure. On the one hand, Hegel distinguishes among three points of view: his own as author and narrator, our point of view as readers and "observers," and the point of view of observed "forms of consciousness." Various "forms of consciousness" (defined and discussed in Chapters 2 and 5) are brought forth to illustrate various philosophical views or theses. Hegel purports that, in his examination, each uncovers problems with its own key ideas through some form of self-critical experience. This expository structure lends Hegel's *Phenomenology* a unique literary cast that, together with the difficulties of identifying within it standard philosophical issues, has suggested to some that his book is primarily literary rather than philosophical. This is an understandable misimpression. Hegel's *Phenomenology* does have a unique literary structure, though Hegel developed it for *philosophical* reasons and purposes. These are discussed in Chapters 2 through 4.

Basic issues that inform Hegel's phenomenological method are introduced in Chapter 2. The expository structure of the *Phenomenology* is further developed in Chapter 3, which shows why key features of Hegel's phenomenological method are modeled on Sophoclean tragedy, most clearly illustrated by Creon's role in *Antigone*. These points are brought together in Chapter 4, which considers the role of philosophical reflection in Hegel's phenomenological method. These three chapters jointly provide the basis for considering the basic features of Hegel's solution to the Dilemma of the Criterion in Chapter 5.

Chapter 6 summarizes some of the main features of Hegel's epistemology. Chapter 7 explores some significant thematic connections between his views and contemporary epistemological problems. With these materials in hand, Hegel's views are considered in relation to twentieth-century empiricism (Chapter 8), Dretske's information theory (Chapter 9), and the continuing debate between realists and historicist relativists (Chapter 10).

One central, recurring theme of this book is the nature and role of reflection in judgment and rational justification. This theme is introduced in Chapter 1, which reviews some basic features of Hegel's "phenomenological" method and his reasons for adopting it. The theme of reflective judgment is raised again at the end of Chapter 2 and developed in Chapter 3, which examines what Hegel very likely learned about it from Sophocles' *Antigone*. Chapter 4 develops this theme further, by highlighting the kind of reflective judgment Hegel seeks to facilitate for and encourage in his readers. The nature and role of reflective judgment in philosophical assessment is expanded in Chapter 5, by linking it to Hegel's analysis of the self-critical structure of self-conscious human awareness. Chapter 5 explicates reflective assessment in terms of "mature judgment" and indicates the role of mature judgment in Hegel's fallibilist account of epistemic justification and his pragmatic account of rationality. In summarizing Hegel's central epistemological arguments in the *Phenomenology*, Chapter 6 indicates how and where Hegel introduces mature judgment as a topic of the *Phenomenology*. Chapters 7 through 10 then invite the reader to consider the nature and role of mature judgment in philosophical assessment by exercising such judgment while reconsidering some central philosophical issues and apparent dilemmas, discussed in these chapters, that have profoundly guided philosophical thought from the Enlightenment to the present day. These include basic assumptions that steered philosophers toward empiricism and individualism in twentieth-century epistemology, or that generated serious misunderstandings that have precluded either recognition or serious philosophical consideration of Hegel's epistemology.

Three specific issues among these are that Hegel anticipated by 150 years the recent rejections in epistemology of concept-empiricism (see §§12, 13.5, 21, 22) and of individualism (§§32ff.). More importantly, Hegel showed how rejecting these positions does not require rejecting epistemological realism about the objects of empirical knowledge. Hegel achieved this insight, in part, by rejecting "internalism" about mental content (§§5, 13.6), semantic meaning (§19), and justification (§§10.2, 10.5, 12.2, 18, 28).[7]

The recent wave of anti-Cartesianism in epistemology and philosophy of mind has much to learn from Hegel. Benefiting from Hegel's insights and analyses, however, requires understanding just what were his aims, methods, and arguments in epistemology. These, however, have eluded most commentators, whether critical or sympathetic. So I begin with Hegel's expository and philosophical methods (§§1–11).

---

7. Section numbers like these are internal references within this book. Section numbers that refer to any other works are preceded by a reference to the relevant work.

The technical terms just used are defined when these issues are discussed in detail in the indicated sections. It should be no surprise that Hegel espoused various "externalist" views, that factors of which someone is unaware affect, e.g., what he or she means, or whether what he or she means is justified. Kant's transcendental analysis of the necessary a priori conditions for the possibility of unified self-conscious experience *is* externalist, *avant la lettre*, because it concerns a set of conditions that must *be* satisfied if and whenever we are self-conscious, regardless of whether we are aware either of these conditions or of their satisfaction.

SECTION 1   5

Please note two caveats, one substantive and one methodological. In focusing this book on Hegel's epistemology in the *Phenomenology* I do not claim that epistemology is his sole concern in the *Phenomenology,* which also includes rich discussions of moral philosophy and Occidental cultural history (including its Oriental roots). Hegel's concern with *Kultur-Kritik* does lend his book many important narrative aspects. These have been analyzed especially well by Henry Harris (1997) in *Hegel's Ladder.*[8] These crucial strands of Hegel's *Phenomenology* ultimately do bear on his epistemology. However, these topics are vast and intricate and can only be touched on in this brief conspectus (mainly in Chapters 9 and 10).

Because this book provides a philosophical overview of some central aspects of Hegel's epistemology, many important points can only be discussed in their barest essentials. I have not shied away from stating the issues and Hegel's stand on them directly. I am keenly aware of the contrast between this approach and the requirements of a full-scale exposition and defense of a philosophical position. I have endeavored to meet those requirements elsewhere, and in parts of the following. Chapters 2 and 5 through 7 are summary in character; the remainder are not. Chapters 3 and 4, on Hegel's method, are entirely new. In Chapters 9 and 10 I consider some important social aspects of Hegel's epistemology much more closely than I have previously.

A full-dress treatment of any significant philosophical issue makes for demanding reading. Understandably, philosophers want and deserve some advance assurance that such reading rewards the effort. This expectation is especially urgent in areas where philosophical rewards are least expected. Notoriously, this is the common view of Hegel's philosophy. I hope that the present introduction, synoptic (even sketchy) as it often is, may help students and nonspecialists to see that studying Hegel is deeply rewarding philosophically, even or especially when it is most philosophically challenging. I hope it may also help Hegel scholars see that Hegel's *Phenomenology* is deeply philosophically rewarding in ways they had not anticipated. Finally, I hope the following may suggest some fruitful ways in which the "Continental" and "Analytic" traditions of philosophy can engage, illuminate, and benefit each other.

Before delving into these rich issues, I might suggest one central thought guiding the vigorous mix of contemporary, historical, analytic, and continental philosophy that is advocated (and I hope also exhibited) in this book: such multiperspectivalism aims to increase our acuity in understanding and assessing philosophical views and thus to mitigate, so far

---

8. For discussion, see Westphal (1998c).

as we are able, a grave professional liability. This liability has been put very well by James Griffin (1996, 2):

> One might succeed in making every argument that one actually deployed watertight. But one does not usually go seriously wrong in philosophy over the details of one's argument. One goes seriously wrong in the biggest things, in the things one does not even think of, in one's whole orientation. At the very best, one's orientation will allow one a glimpse of an important truth or two, but it will also certainly be responsible for one's overlooking a dozen others. In philosophy generally . . . we are at present, and always shall be, groping in the dark simply to get a sense of some of the large contours of our subject. One's only reasonable hope is that, by groping, one will find something, and that others will take a look.

In a notoriously fractious field, we can all benefit by this kind of inquiring modesty, which whets the appetite for philosophy far more than do faction and favoritism.

Two

Introducing Hegel's Phenomenological Method

2 Hegel's phenomenological method is so unusual that it and its origins cry out for explanation. Several philosophical issues and sources help elucidate some important features of Hegel's phenomenological method. These are discussed in the present chapter. Chapter 3 provides some essential literary background to Hegel's method and exposition. Chapter 4 draws these two strands together to provide some conclusions regarding Hegel's phenomenological method.

2.1 The best single sentence about Hegel's phenomenological method was written by Jonathan Robinson (1977, 2), who observed:

> The full strength of Hegel's position [in the *Phenomenology*] is appreciated only when it is understood that he is arguing that bad theory makes for bad practice, and that the bad practice shows up the logical difficulties of the theory.

Robinson highlights the important fact that Hegel's *Phenomenology* considers philosophical issues, views, and principles, not in abstraction, but in close connection with their intended uses for comprehending their intended range of phenomena (*ta phainòmena*, in Aristotle's sense), including the opinions of the many and the wise. More importantly, Robinson's statement stresses that Hegel's phenomenological method critically assesses philosophical views by considering carefully the ways in which and the extent to which the intended use of philosophical principles substantiates, qualifies, or undermines them. Hegel's phenomenological method involves a dialectical juxtaposition of principles and the actual practices they purport to guide, by exhibiting them for our benefit in the figure and actions of their paradigmatic exponent. Uniquely, the internal critique central to Hegel's method is not driven by an interlocutor; it is driven by the very proponent of the relevant principles him- or herself, though the proponent's self-criticism is presented for the benefit and insight of an audience consisting of Hegel's readers. What makes this dialectic "phenomenological"?

One important clue to Hegel's unique style of phenomenology comes from the title of the last chapter of Kant's *Metaphysical Foundations of*

Natural Science, "Phenomenology." In that chapter Kant examines the metaphysical principles undergirding Newton's efforts to determine the true locations and motions (orbits) of the planets, based on observational data regarding their apparent locations and motions. Analogously, Hegel's *Phenomenology* examines a series of "forms of consciousness" (*Gestalten des Bewußtseins*). "Forms of consciousness" are apparent or putative forms of knowledge. (Later in the *Phenomenology,* these forms of consciousness are also forms of practical agency; Hegel contends that knowledge is rooted in practice.) The forms of consciousness Hegel considers in the *Phenomenology* are based on various ways in which human knowledge appears, both in the expressions and behavior of the many and in the theories of the philosophically wise. All of these appearances are, Hegel believes, more or less adequate and more or less accurate manifestations of our actual cognitive capacities and abilities, and of the actual objects and events we engage through those capacities and abilities. These forms of apparent knowledge manifest, to some degree and in some way or ways, our actual cognitive situation because they are rooted, however distantly, in our actual cognitive situation. Hegel's careful, detailed, internal critique of these forms of apparent knowledge aims to enable us ultimately to grasp the nature and scope of true or genuine knowledge, which concludes his book.

Hegel's use of the term "absolute" deserves comment. Hegel defines genuine or "absolute" knowledge in the first sentence of the *Phenomenology* as "*das wirkliche Erkennen dessen, was in Wahrheit ist*": "the actual knowledge of what in truth is" (*PhdG* 9:53). This phrase specifies Hegel's meaning of his term "*das Absolute,*" which Hegel sets in apposition to this phrase later in this same sentence. In these introductory remarks he does not, and is not entitled to, take any particular stand on what ultimately there is "in truth." The remainder of his first paragraph (indeed, the remainder of the *Phenomenology*) sustains this use and meaning of "absolute." The common assumption that "absolute" is supposed to modify grammatically *how* we know "what in truth is" is spurious and imports the common epistemological fixation on "certainty" into Hegel's *Phenomenology,* which in fact gets his views backwards. Hegel repeatedly analyzes various "certainties" in the *Phenomenology.* These certainties are antecedent convictions about what there is and how or whether we know what there is (or, in practice, can achieve what we intend). Hegel examines these "certainties" in order to expose them as premature and at least somewhat erroneous convictions that, however insightful or informative, cannot ultimately be justified.

Reading Hegel effectively requires taking to heart Frege's lesson that the meaning of any word is only determinate within a sentence. Most importantly, Frege's lesson concerns *each* sentence individually in which a term occurs (Conant 2002, 384–5, 398–9). Hegel is *the* past master of contextually defining and redefining key terms as their context of use is developed. Thus his texts must also be read with sensitivity to Carnap's (1956, 49–52) related point that the meaning of a term is specified by identifying which inferences can, and which cannot, be drawn using that term. Assimilating Hegel's terms to other familiar usage is guaranteed to confuse and obscure. Unfortunately, this has too often been the fate of Hegel's readers.

A third important characteristic of Hegel's phenomenological dialectic derives from his concern to avoid the five skeptical modes of Agrippa (infinite regress, relativity, assumption, circularity, and discrepancy).[1] Hegel avoids these five modes by solving the Pyrrhonian Dilemma of the Criterion (below, Chapter 5). Hegel's solution to this Dilemma involves a subtle and powerful analysis of the possibility of constructive self-criticism. According to Hegel, human consciousness has a self-critical structure, regardless of whether we acknowledge or exploit it. Hegel purports to exhibit our self-critical capacity in the structure and behavior of the "forms of consciousness" examined in his *Phenomenology*. Hegel aims to avoid begging the question by supporting his own positive philosophical conclusions solely on the basis of an internal critique of opposed philosophical views. This is an extremely demanding requirement, which Hegel fulfills astonishingly well.

2.2   Each form of consciousness is guided by a basic pair of conceptions: a conception of itself as a form of consciousness, either cognitive or practical, and a conception of its proper object or objects. I use the term "conception" in order to denote conceptual representations that individuals use, know, and can master. Hegel uses the term "*Begriff*" ("concept") also to designate objective structures in the natural world (see §12.5). Distinguishing these two ideas terminologically helps clarify Hegel's view. (Philosophical German recently adopted the Anglicism "*Konzeption*" to remedy precisely this want in philosophical usage.)

Hegel's phenomenological method treats these pairs of conceptions as instantiated in and used by a representative "form of consciousness" in

---

1. *PH* I §§164–9. "Discrepancy" concerns "interminable conflict [both among ordinary people and philosophers] because of which we are unable to choose a thing or reject it, and so fall back on suspension" (*PH* I §165). On the importance of the Five Modes of Agrippa within contemporary epistemology, see Westphal (1989a), chs. 4, 5; (1998b); and Fogelin (1994). For a concise synopsis of Pyrrhonian skepticism, see Westphal (1989a), 11–6.

order to consider these conceptions not abstractly but in their use for comprehending or acting on the objects or phenomena each form of consciousness contends exists and purports adequately to understand, including understanding itself by using its self-conception. Considering each form of consciousness' conceptions in their use *in concreto* allows Hegel's phenomenological method to consider the *experience* generated by each form of consciousness. Each form of consciousness generates its experience by using its lead conceptions to grasp and grapple with its purported objects. Because each form of consciousness' experience is structured *both* by its lead conceptions *and* by the objects regarding which each form of consciousness uses those conceptions, if those conceptions do not correspond to their objects, then they also do not correspond to the experience a form of consciousness has of its object, or of itself. The critical point of Hegel's method is to exploit these discrepancies in order to develop the most sophisticated version of each form of consciousness, and to determine whether the most sophisticated version of a form of consciousness is ultimately adequate to its intended domain. (These points are discussed in greater detail in Chapter 5.)

2.3 Hegel's critique of forms of consciousness is internal; it considers only, for each form of consciousness, its key conceptions and its experience of its intended domain. For this reason, his phenomenological presentation acquires a dramatic structure unparalleled in the history of philosophy. In this literary regard, the closest philosophical work would be Rousseau's *Confessions,* in which each of the three dramatis personae represent by turns various aspects of the author and confessor himself, Rousseau. However, these three points of view have a very different purpose and structure from those found in Hegel's *Phenomenology*. The dramatic structure of Hegel's *Phenomenology* involves three concurrent and coordinated points of view: his point of view as author and narrator (prominent in introductory, transitional, and summary passages); the point of view of his readers, who are to learn about and from forms of consciousness by "observing" them; and the point of view represented by each specific form of consciousness. Why does Hegel use this elaborate expository structure? One important reason is that Hegel's primary philosophical lessons are to be learned by his readers, the observing "we." Whether any particular form of consciousness learns these lessons is a distinct question; often they don't, even if they uncover sufficient information to do so.

One important philosophical reason for Hegel to distinguish among these three points of view can be understood by considering the distinction between a sound argument and a proof. A logically *valid* argument is one whose conclusion follows from its premises, on pain of contradiction. A logically *sound* argument is a logically valid argument that has true premises. By themselves, however, sound arguments don't provide knowledge. To provide knowledge, the premises of a sound argument must be *known* (and the validity of the argument must be recognized). If the premises of a sound argument are known, the argument in question is a *proof.* Thus a proof is a sound argument the premises of which are known to be true. In philosophical disputes, the distinction between sound arguments and proofs poses a vital issue: a sound argument provides knowledge only for those who know the premises and grasp its validity. In disputed philosophical domains, the key premises of an argument or the inferences it uses typically are disputed; at least one party to the debate denies that one or more premises are true, or denies that one or another inference is valid, and so does not and cannot base any knowledge on that argument. What can be done to address this problem? What can we do if we offer someone a genuine proof, though she or he rejects it or just doesn't "get it"?

2.4 Kant recognized that we cannot base philosophical proofs on self-evident truths. Any genuinely self-evident truths belong to logic or mathematics, though these do not entail the truth of any substantive philosophical conclusions. Even Kant's own "apodictic" (Bxxii, note 2) transcendental proofs of the necessary conditions for the possibility of unified self-conscious experience are not based on self-evident truths. Instead, Kant's transcendental proofs are based on an inventory of our basic human cognitive capacities and consequent *in*capacities. Kant proposed to identify our basic cognitive capacities and incapacities by providing a series of striking thought experiments. As Kant's readers, we are to consider his thought experiments carefully and reflectively to determine as honestly and accurately as we are able whether we in fact have the cognitive capacities and incapacities Kant claimed to identify (Westphal 2003c). In this way, Kant's method relies on mutual critical assessment to establish our basic list of cognitive capacities and incapacities (O'Neill 1992). Our careful, reflective consideration of Kant's illuminating counterexamples involves a general version of what Kant called "transcendental reflection" (B316–7; Westphal 2003c).[2]

---

2. Kant scholars may suspect a tension here between the kind of indirect proof inherently involved in arguing by counterexamples and Kant's repudiation of indirect proof in his Transcendental Doctrine of Method (A789–91/B817–9). The tension is more apparent than real. Kant does argue directly from the principles of his transcendental analyses, but to establish those principles Kant typically argues by *modus tollens,* on the basis of telling, wildly counterfactual exam-

Hegel was the first philosopher to do what has become commonplace among analytic Kant scholars, namely, to reject Kant's transcendental idealism while retaining and emphasizing his "transcendental" analysis of the necessary a priori conditions for unified self-conscious experience. Because Hegel disagreed fundamentally with Kant's transcendental idealism, he also rejected Kant's transcendental idealist account of our basic cognitive capacities. To replace these, Hegel explicated a much more elaborate set of social and historical conditions necessary for individual cognitive judgment, a set that incorporated many of Kant's most important theses (while revising or even dispensing with Kant's accounts of them). The complexities of these issues, the difficulties confronting our careful, honest, and constructive reflection on our own cognitive capacities, and especially the problem of reaching agreement about which among a myriad of claims about our basic cognitive capacities are in fact true led Hegel to expand Kant's notion of transcendental reflection and to incorporate it into his phenomenological dialectic. How did he do this? How did he get the idea that this could be done?

2.5 In Hegel's *Phenomenology,* the central figures are forms of consciousness, which we—Hegel's readers—are to "observe" and carefully consider during our critical self-examination. Hegel's phenomenological method centrally involves these seven features:

1. It exhibits and uses internal self-criticism in a narratively constructed figure or character;
2. Through this self-criticism the character him- or herself uncovers the central critical problems with his or her favored views;
3. These central critical problems are discovered through his or her own *use* and *development in practice* of his or her key principles and claims;
4. These results purportedly suffice to refute those principles and claims;
5. These results are exhibited for an observing audience in all their graphic and telling detail;

---

ples. (One example of this is discussed here in §15.) In the *Methodenlehre,* Kant cautions against indirect proof of any kind of philosophical "hypothesis," while affirming the validity of *modus tollens*. In the second edition Preface, Kant insists that his transcendental analyses do not rely on hypotheses (Bxxii, note).

6. These results purportedly suffice to justify introducing a more sophisticated successor view;

7. This successor view purports to incorporate the insights and remedy the oversights of the refuted view.

I believe that there are no philosophical models for this central complex of features of Hegel's phenomenological method.[3] Might Hegel's method draw from a model outside philosophy? Does the dramatic structure of the *Phenomenology* suggest perhaps a literary model? I believe so, for reasons explored in the next chapter.

---

3. None is familiar to me from extensive research in the history of philosophy, nor is any suggested by the entries on "*Phänomenologie*" in Sandkühler (1990), Mittelstraß (1980, 2001), or Ritter and Gründer (1971).

THREE

Internal Critique in Sophocles' *Antigone*

3. A Literary Model of Hegel's Philosophical Method

Sophocles' *Antigone* is a direct forbearer to Hegel's phenomenological method. Whether it was his own model, or only illustrates some key features of his phenomenology, I do not know, nor do I know how to determine whether it was. We know, however, that Hegel greatly admired Greek tragedy and this play in particular. This chapter examines how *Antigone* models some core features, both literary and philosophical, of Hegel's phenomenological method. The key parallels are both central and striking enough to lend significant credibility to my suggestion.[1]

4. Creon as a Form of Consciousness

Antigone presents a model of internal, phenomenological critique, especially through the figure of Creon.[2] In his first speech upon ascending to the throne, Creon emphasizes the gravity and self-disclosure involved in

---

1. My suggestion may easily provoke alternative suggestions, for which I would be very grateful. However, any alternative suggestion must make good sense of both the literary and the philosophical structure of Hegel's *Phenomenology*. On this latter point, see Westphal (1989a).

2. My interpretation and use of *Antigone* is indebted to Nussbaum (1986), ch. 3, which is recommended background for the present discussion. Please note that the content of the play discussed here does not pertain to the content that is central to Hegel's own analysis of *Antigone* in the "Spirit" section of the *Phenomenology*. On Hegel's own analysis of *Antigone,* see Westphal (1989a), 174–8, and Ferrini (2002).

Readers may wonder whether the following interpretation of Creon's role in *Antigone* is actually in Sophocles' play or would only be apparent to Hegel when reading it, due to his concerns about self-criticism. I believe I provide ample evidence that the play does present an internal critique of Creon's position. If readers remain unconvinced of this, it suffices for my claim about Hegel that *Antigone* is relevant to his method in the ways I indicate, even if Hegel could or did recognize these features of *Antigone* only in view of his own methodological concerns with self-criticism.

ruling and legislating (175–7).³ He insists that a ruler must say and do what is right. Immediately he rejects favoritism in any form and identifies the safety of the polis as the supreme good and sine qua non for all other goods (175–91, 209–10). Creon's identification of individual good with the good of the polis, where the good of the polis is identified solely with its safety, is a portentous innovation.

As a direct corollary to this declaration, Creon forbids, on pain of death (220–1), the burial of the corpse of Polynices (198–208). Common Attic policy was to return enemy corpses to their compatriots for burial and removing traitors' corpses beyond the precinct of the polis, leaving them unburied.⁴ Beyond the district of the polis, traitors' corpses could be collected either by family or by compatriots for proper, if private, burial. To the Greeks, burial was an essential religious rite, necessary to allow the departed's passage to Hades. Creon's edict forbidding Polynices' burial is a second portentous innovation. It appears that Creon recognized his innovations, since he introduced them with such gravity and care on what was already a very grave occasion.⁵ The Chorus recognize that siding with anyone who disobeys Creon's edict would be punished by death (220). Significantly, in response to their observation, Creon indicates his obsession with insubordination and bribery (222).

Creon's concise, express presentation of his ruling principles and their consequences for policy corresponds exactly to Hegel's introductory presentation of the core principles of a form of consciousness at the beginning of each chapter of the *Phenomenology,* and of each major phase within any chapter. Sophocles' audience can already see that Creon errs, as do most Thebans represented in *Antigone.* However, Creon has already set up one of his greatest defenses against dissent, even in the form of respectful constructive criticism: his immediate suspicion and charge of bribery. Creon's repeated and impatient use of this standard retort cuts him off from anyone's corrective advice.⁶ Thus the question is: Can anything

---

3. References to *Antigone* (Sophocles 2001) are by standard line ("verse") numbers. Readers unfamiliar with *Antigone* may also enjoy the excellent video production of it directed by George Tzavella (Sophocles 1962).
4. Cf. Napolitano Valditara (2002), note 40, and Nussbaum (1986), 55, 437–8, note 14.
5. Cf. Nussbaum (1986), 56.
6. Including, especially, Antigone's. Thus, even though Creon confronts other agents in ways that forms of consciousness need not, and often do not, Creon's stubborn refusal to listen until he is driven to do so by fate underwrites the internality of Sophocles' critique of Creon in *Antigone.*

lead Creon to recognize his errors? Can Creon come to see his own errors? Indeed so: the main events presented in *Antigone* serve as an internal critique of Creon's ruling principles, but only by taking them in connection with Creon's thoughts and actions as they guide his implementation of his ruling principles and practices. Creon's principles, policies, and practices present a "form of consciousness," in Hegel's sense. From Creon's initial declarations ensue a whole array of increasingly urgent, even terrifying incidents and attempts to get the point through Creon's stubborn head. His self-confident refusal to listen ensures that the full and terrible consequences of his narrow-minded ruling principles will be explored and articulated in all their excruciating detail, until even he finds cause (if not at first reason) to recant his disastrous principles and edict.

Identifying the character of Creon as an instance of an Hegelian "form of consciousness" is clinched by this striking fact. When Hegel introduces a form of consciousness, he identifies its key principles as the "certainty" of this form of consciousness. These principles articulate that what this form of consciousness is "certain" of are the key features of both itself and its objects (Westphal 1989a, 92). Analogously, Creon's single-minded self-confidence in his key principles and policies indicate unequivocally that he is utterly certain that they represent what good ruling is all about.

There is more to this key parallel. Within any chapter of Hegel's *Phenomenology*, the development of one form of consciousness typically runs through three phases. A form of consciousness' initial certainty generates difficulties in the first phase. These lead it to refine, qualify, and shift its main principles (its "certainty") for the second phase, though its revised view again generates difficulties. The third phase then considers the most sophisticated and adequate version of this form of consciousness and again purports to generate difficulties within it. Purportedly, these difficulties are so severe that the entire form of consciousness must be revoked. Each subsequent form of consciousness preserves each predecessor's insights while correcting their errors. This is Hegel's sense of "*Aufhebung*," which is rendered in English by "sublation," an archaic term retained in order to mean what Hegel means by "*Aufhebung*": to cancel or nullify, to preserve, and to raise up. Hegel's internal critique purports to identify and nullify the errors while preserving the insights of a view (held by a form of consciousness) by incorporating those insights, suitably revised, within a more sophisticated and adequate view (held by a successor form of consciousness).

A striking feature of Creon's behavior in *Antigone* is that, once severe troubles arise from his original declarations, he revises and qualifies his views in significant ways. In fact, he does this twice. Each time his views become more extreme but also more entrenched and less open to criticism—until finally even he is driven to recognize his errors and to recant his innovative principles and policies.

5. The Internal Critique of Creon's Form of Consciousness in *Antigone*

Consider Creon's form of consciousness more closely. As mentioned, Creon announces clearly and carefully his innovative principles and policies—his "certainty," in Hegel's terminology—when he first ascends to the Theban throne. He is entirely confident that he correctly grasps the essence of good ruling, and that using his principles will guide Thebes rightly and safely through the turbulence of Greek political life. He soon has occasion to reaffirm his certainty about their correctness. When the Watchman arrives with the terrible news that Polynices has been ritually buried, Creon automatically retorts that the Watchman was bribed (293–304, 310–2, 322, 326). When to the contrary the Chorus for the first time very cautiously suggest that perhaps the gods favored this ritual burial (278–9), Creon rebukes them and adamantly denies that gods could care at all for a traitor's corpse (282–3). Significantly, Creon suggests a revision of his principles of political governance, obliquely identifying his rule with justice itself (289–92). (This oblique suggestion is soon made explicit.) The Watchman is the second to suggest, very cautiously, that Creon's judgment is misguided: "It's terrible when false judgment guides the judge" (323). Creon of course will have none of this (324).

The importance of these points about Creon's rule is soon underscored for the audience by the Chorus, who remark on the general issues involved:

> If he honors the law of the land
> And the oath-bound justice of the gods,
> Then his city shall stand high.
> But no city for him if he turns shameless out of daring.
> He will be no guest of mine,
> He will never share my thoughts,
> If he goes wrong. (369–75)

The intended object of the Chorus' admonition is not specified.[7] However, it fits Creon's rule. Creon's initial declarations and edicts were daring, he now rules Thebes, and he's about to reassert *his* law of the land, utterly rejecting Antigone's reverence for "the oath-bound justice of the

---

7. For discussion, see Napolitano Valditara (2002), notes 13, 35.

gods." The Chorus thus forewarn the audience about the evident and impending implications of Creon's innovative certainty.

When brought before Creon, Antigone accepts the charges against her (443, 449). However, when Creon asks Antigone whether she dared to violate his laws, she underscores the general point made by the Chorus (369–72), which they had cautiously raised in connection with Creon's edict (278–9), and makes this point explicit to Creon: she retorts directly that no human law can override divine law. Indeed, she denies that Creon's edicts were either law or justice:

> What laws? I never heard it was Zeus
> Who made that announcement.
> And it wasn't justice, either. The gods below
> Didn't lay down this law for human use.
> And I never thought your announcements
> Could give you—a mere human being—
> Power to trample the gods' unfailing,
> Unwritten laws. These laws weren't made now
> Or yesterday. They live for all time,
> And no one knows when they came into the light.
> No man could frighten me into taking on
> The gods' penalty for breaking such a law.   (450–60)[8]

Significantly, the Chorus comment on Antigone's rigidity: "She has no idea how to bow her head to trouble" (472). Creon amplifies this point to the Chorus:

> Don't forget: The mind that is most rigid
> Stumbles soonest; the hardest iron—
> Tempered in fire till it is super-strong—
> Shatters easily and clatters into shards.
> And you can surely break the wildest horse
> With a tiny bridle. . . .   (473–8)

---

8. This speech is one of the earliest extant statements of the natural law position that there are normative standards of justice that transcend human edict, statutory law, or agreed convention (Napolitano Valditara 2002, §B and note 43; Ostwald 1973). This is significant for Hegel's analysis of *Antigone* in the *Phenomenology*. The idea of natural law is essentially critical, for it concerns *standards* of political legitimacy that are valid independent of human beliefs, edicts, or institutions, and which can be used to assess their legitimacy. Hegel too belongs to the natural law tradition (Westphal 2003d).

In this way, the play makes explicit the contrast between flexibility and rigid adherence to rules, consequences be damned. It is not long before Haemon raises this issue directly about, and *to,* his father, Creon.

To Creon's charge that Antigone alone favors burying Polynices (508), Antigone replies that the whole of Thebes agrees with her, though Creon has silenced them (504–7, 509). Creon of course rejects her claim, just as he rejected the earlier, analogous suggestion by the Chorus (278–83). Creon now reveals his second defense strategy: he refuses to be "ruled by a woman" (484–5, 525). When sentencing Antigone to death, Ismene and the Chorus all remind him that prima facie there are further relevant considerations: for example, Antigone is betrothed to Creon's son, Haemon (568–75). Having drawn the direct syllogistic conclusion of his policy, upon finding the instance to which it applies, namely to the guilty Antigone, Creon directly rejects any suggestion that Antigone is a suitable bride for Haemon (571, 650–4). Nussbaum (1986, 57–8, 61) nicely brings out how callous is Creon's reasoning.

In the Second Stasimon, the Chorus reiterate the tragic law of Zeus:

> And this will be the law,
> Now and for time to come, as it was before:
> Madness stalks mortals who are great,
> Leaves no escape from disaster.   (611–4)

The Chorus directly link this law with "Those who judge that crime is good . . . " (621–5). The immediate reference would appear to be to Antigone, who violated Creon's edict and thought it good to do so. Ultimately, the play makes clear that Creon is doomed to this madness (1257–60).

Haemon enters, approaching his father solicitously (635–8). Creon responds by praising Haemon's obeisance, stating that a proper son "will punish his father's enemies / And reward his friends—as his father would" (643–4). This is a curious and striking premonition of what Creon soon says about ruling the polis. After reiterating the death sentence he passed on Antigone, Creon declares:

> The public knows that a man is just
> Only if he is straight with his relatives.   (661–2)

In this way Creon recalls the first theme of his ascension speech, about public knowledge of his ruling principles and character (175–7). In precisely that vein, he continues:

So, if someone goes too far and breaks the law,
Or tries to tell his masters what to do,
He will have nothing but contempt from me. (663–5)

We have begun to see just how widely Creon distributes his scorn and contempt! Note that he continues expounding his ruling principles, but now with a very significant shift. He now says:

... when the city takes a leader, you must obey,
Whether his commands are trivial, or right, or wrong.
And I have no doubt that such a man will rule well,
And, later, he will cheerfully be ruled by someone else. (666–9)

... when people stay in line and obey,
Their lives and everything else are safe.
For this reason, order must be maintained ... (675–7)

In his ascension speech, Creon identified right with the safety of the polis (184–91). Narrow as this equation is, it does allow for a criterion of the justice of a ruler's edicts, namely, whether those edicts in fact serve—indeed, maximally serve—the safety of the polis. Now Creon equates right action with total obedience, even if the ruler's commands are wrong! This stops just short of equating right with whatever a ruler declares by edict, but it does identify obedience to justice with obedience to the ruler's command. Significantly, the only alternative Creon can envisage to utter obedience is anarchy (672–4). Debate or reconsideration are completely beyond his pale, such is his rigidity (i.e., "certainty"). Maintaining order requires, apparently above all else, "no surrender to a woman" (678–80).

It is important to see that Creon's phrase about obedience "right or wrong" is authentic. In part, Creon only follows the earlier invitation of the Chorus, who said of his edict, "it's up to you: / Make any law you want—for the dead, or for us who live" (213–4). The authenticity of Creon's new principle is directly supported by his imminent retrenchment of his position (738, discussed below), which directly supports this surprising principle.

The Chorus credit Creon with speaking well (681–2), though soon they say the same of Haemon after he beseeches his father (725). Haemon beseeches his father as gently and obeisantly as possible, suggesting that if Creon has misspoken, he doubts that he (Haemon) can clarify this point, though perhaps someone else might (683–7). Haemon recognizes that, as Creon's son, he is naturally obliged to watch out for his father's well-being, and that he has a special role to play in this regard, since ordinary people wouldn't risk saying openly anything that might offend Creon (688–91).[9] Haemon immediately confirms Thebes' grief over Antigone and the injustice of her fate (693–700). He warns Creon against the hazards of close-mindedness (706–9, cf. 720–3), suggesting that

> ... a wise man can learn a lot and never be ashamed;
> He knows he does not have to be rigid and close-hauled. (710–1)

Haemon then echoes earlier metaphors of the danger of rigidity used by the Chorus (472) and by Creon himself (473–8), this time with the image of stiff trees ruined by flash floods (712–4) and boats capsized by holding the sail too close (715–7). Haemon concludes by respectfully suggesting that Creon should relax and reconsider. The Chorus endorse both speeches and recommend that father and son alike should learn from each other (724–5).

So certain is Creon of his principles and policies that he utterly rejects Haemon's speech, accusing him of "breaking ranks"—very nearly a charge he made against Antigone (730, cf. 510). In their escalating exchange, Creon fatefully recasts his ruling principle:

> I should rule this country for someone other than myself? (736)
>
> A city belongs to its master. Isn't that the rule? (738)

This principle differs dramatically from Creon's initial identification of justice with the safety of the polis. Indeed, this very nearly implies that the safety of the city is only good for the sake of the ruler. Between Creon's insistence on obedience above all else, and now his bald assertion that a city belongs to its *master* (not ruler), there is every reason to think that Creon would insist, as he did earlier, on obedience right or wrong (666–7).

Haemon easily sees the madness of such principles, which he highlights by stating:

> A place for one man alone is not a city. (737)
>
> Then go be ruler of a desert, all alone. You'd do it well. (739)
>
> ... All I'm saying is, you haven't thought this through. (753)

---

9. The Watchman's reluctance to bring Creon the news of Polynices' ritual burial (223–36, 243, 270–7) shows keen awareness of this risk.

If you weren't my father I'd say you were out of your mind. (755)[10]

Talk, talk, talk! Why don't you ever want to listen? (757)

In reply to Creon's charge that Haemon is accusing his own father (742), Haemon replies:

Because I see you going wrong. Because justice matters! (743)
You have no respect at all if you trample on the rights of gods! (745)

In this way, Haemon takes up both Antigone's and the Chorus' point about the crucial importance of divine law (369–75, 455). However, all Creon can see in Haemon's speech is his insubordination and siding with a woman (725–6, 730, 734, 740, 742, 744, 746, 748, 752, 756). The first and very slight indication given by Creon that he can reconsider something is his agreement with the Chorus that Ismene should not be punished (770–1).

As Antigone is led to her cave, the Chorus appear to confirm the glory, if not quite the justice, of her cause (cf. 854–5, 872–5).[11] They contrast their own mortality to Antigone's (834–5) and declare of her,

... when you die, you will be great,
You will be equal in memory to the gods,
By the glory of your life and death. (836–8, cf. 817–22)

---

10. This is the first direct suggestion that the madness characterized earlier by the Chorus (611–4) may pertain to Creon.

11. Though Antigone rejects the Chorus' declaration as sarcastic irony (839–43), their declaration accords entirely with Antigone's original insistence that the whole of Thebes agrees with her burial of Polynices (504–7, 509); the Chorus' original suggestion that Polynices' ceremonial burial may have been divine (278–9); Haemon's reports of Theban opinion (692–700, 731–3) and his statement that Creon earns only disrespect by trampling the laws of the gods (745, cf. 743); the Chorus' urgent advice given as soon as Creon is willing to listen (1098–107); Tiresias' advice and prophecy (1014–22, 1029–31, 1065–83); the Chorus' stress on the infallibility of Tiresias' prophecies, which Creon confirms (1092–5); Eurydice's condemnation of Creon (1305, 1313); and the Chorus' final speech (1348–53), which directly comments on Creon (1338–47, cf. 1257–69). Given all the evidence supporting this major theme, honoring Antigone's burial of her brother, despite Creon's edict, shows instead that in her distress Antigone has seriously mistaken the point of the Chorus' praises. Note too that her mistake is made in ignorance of each of these clear indicators that her original insistence was indeed correct. (This note anticipates topics discussed just below.)

Creon still refuses to see this side of the situation.

Then Tiresias has occasion to make essentially the same point. He insists that Creon's edict brought a plague of pollution down upon the altars of Thebes (1014–22). He underscores and amplifies Haemon's point about the perils of rigidity:

> It's common knowledge, any human being can go wrong.
> But even when he does, a man may still succeed:
> He may have his share of luck and good advice
> But only if he's willing to bend and find a cure
> For the trouble he's caused. It's only being stubborn
> Proves you're a fool. . . . (1024–9)

Tiresias directly advises Creon:

> . . . surrender to the dead man.
> Stop stabbing away at his corpse. Will it prove your strength
> If you kill him again? Listen, my advice is for your benefit. (1029–31)

Thus the prophet directly recommends surrendering Polynices to Hades by granting his burial.

Before hearing Tiresias' prophecy, Creon extols the supreme value of Tiresias' advice (993, 995). In reply to his prophecy, Creon immediately retorts as usual, accusing all soothsayers of utter greed (1035–8, 1046–8, 1055, 1061–3).[12] Tiresias recognizes that Creon's retort implies that he, Tiresias, makes false prophecies (1054). He remarks,

> How powerful good judgment is, compared to wealth. (1050)

Creon concurs and adds:

> . . . And no harm compares with heedlessness. (1051)

Tiresias rejoins:

> Which runs through you [Creon] like the plague. (1052)[13]

---

12. This also, if indirectly, corroborates ascribing to Creon the principle of obedience, right or wrong (666–7).

13. Creon's "heedlessness," here stressed expressly by Tiresias, underwrites the internality of Sophocles' critique of Creon's position.

Tiresias parries the charge of greed, redounding it on Creon and—finally!—explicitly identifies the tyranny of Creon's rule (1066). Creon insists that he is commander in chief (1057) and explicitly refuses to change his mind (1063). Creon's defiant rebuke to Tiresias underscores how convinced Creon is that justice is a matter of obeying a ruler's commands, right or wrong (666–7).

Now utterly provoked, Tiresias reveals his most fearsome prophecy, which echoes Haemon's remark to Creon that Antigone's death would result in another death (751). Tiresias now foretells that, because Creon's edict was "violence" against Polynices, Antigone, and the gods (1068–73), less than a day will pass before Creon's last remaining son will perish (1066–7) and that Creon shall be "tangled in the net of [his] own crimes" (1076). Tiresias thus confirms the justice of Antigone's act. His parting remarks comment on Creon:

> May he learn to cultivate a gentler tongue
> And a mind more cogent than he has shown today. (1089–90)

The Chorus stress Tiresias' infallible record, which Creon confirms (1092–5).

Finally, Creon's "mind is shaken" (1095). Finally, he recognizes that either of his options, conceding or persisting, is awe-ful (*deinon;* 1096–7).[14]

The Chorus stress one of Tiresias' (1050), and indeed one of Haemon's (705–23) key points:

> Good judgment is essential, Creon. Take advice. (1098)

For the first time, Creon is willing to take advice, though he remains oblivious to the obvious:

> What should I do? Show me. I'll do what you say. (1099)

Now permitted to speak, the Chorus tell him the obvious, which they have been trying to tell him from the beginning (278–9): that Antigone should be released and Polynices buried (1100–1). Creon is astonished (1102) and indicates that he has hardly changed his views at all:

---

14. Nussbaum (1986, 52) notes that "*deinon*" has a wide range of connotation: generally used of something that elicits awe or wonder, it can also be used of dazzling intellectual brilliance, monstrous evil, or the terrible power of fate. If we took the English term "awful" literally, it would serve to render "*deinon*."

Section 5

> It's so painful to pull back; it goes against my heart.
> But I cannot fight against necessity. (1105–6)

Claiming that his mind is finally changed, he hurries to release Antigone (1111–2). Only now does Creon make a crucial concession, directly repudiating the innovations that he made in his ascension speech:

> I'm afraid it is best to obey the laws,
> Just as tradition has them, all one's life. (1113–4)

Without giving her credit, Creon finally admits the justice of Antigone's original claim on behalf of timeless, unwritten customary *cum* divine law. This admission implicitly concedes that he cannot simply make any law he likes (cf. 214). However, Creon's concession is qualified. His mind is changed by necessity (as he says), not by insight. Now he merely follows orders, by doing what the Chorus tell him to do. Unfortunately, it is too late; fate has taken over, and the horrifying turns of the final events are now inevitable. What matters now is to note how the essential lessons to be learned from Creon's key ruling principles are stressed in the closing scenes. The guard who brings the terrible news of Haemon's death to the court concludes his report to the Queen by saying that all of this

> ... proves the point: In a human life,
> It's deadly for bad judgment to embrace a man. (1242–3)

Upon returning with Haemon's body, Creon excoriates himself:

> Oh, howl for the sins of a stubborn mind,
> Evil-minded, death-dealing! ... (1261–2)

> Cry out against the sacrilege that I called strategy! (1265)

> You [Haemon] were expelled from life
> By my bad judgment, never yours. (1268–9)

The Chorus confirm:

> Yes, it is late, but you have seen where justice lies. (1270)

Creon admits:

> Oh yes:
> I have learned, and it is misery. (1271–2)

Now Creon rightly claims—and is rightly credited with—learning, with understanding and insight.[15] Then he learns of his wife's, Eurydice's, suicide. As Nussbaum (1986, 62) notes, her name literally means "wide justice." Her suicide etches the point that Creon's rigidity *is* the death of "wide justice," or justice in an inclusive, considerate sense. At death, Eurydice as "inclusive justice" condemns Creon, charging:

"These are your crimes, Childkiller!" (1305)

"You're to blame for his death, and the other boy's, too." (1313)

Dissolved in misery (1311, 1343), Creon confesses his crimes (1339–42) and admits:

I am worth less than a nobody. (1325)

This, from a man who so confidently ascended to the throne of Thebes only two days prior! The Chorus conclude:

Wisdom [*Phronein*] is supreme for a blesséd life [*eudaimonia*],
And reverence for the gods
Must never cease.
Great words, sprung from arrogance,
Are punished by great blows.
So it is one learns, in old age, to be wise. (1348–53)

6. Summary of the Internal Critique of Creon in *Antigone*

As Thebes celebrated its victory over Polynices' invading army, rejoicing in its safety and security, Creon assumed the throne and introduced some key innovations that were directed solely to the safety and security of the polis. However well-intentioned, his innovations instead led Thebes to the brink of an even greater disaster than the military defeat it had just avoided. By violating divine law, Creon's innovative principles and policies led directly, not to Thebes' security but to its near collapse. Through their consistent and persistent execution, Creon's innovations have refuted themselves. None of his revisions or retrenchments sufficed to secure his certainty against critical assessment or self-refutation.

Initially, Creon equates good with the safety of the polis (175–91, 209–10). As a corollary to this, he denies any honors to traitors such as

---

15. Cf. Ferrini (2002), §E.

Polynices (198–208). In the face of mounting difficulties, Creon then insists that justice lies in obedience to one's ruler, right or wrong (666–9, cf. 289–92). When this retrenchment of his principles generates further difficulties, he insists that "a city belongs to its master" and that he is entitled to rule the city as he sees fit (736, 738). These principles all founder on the fact that the good of the city is complex, so that ruling for the sake of the good of the polis requires taking this complexity of civil goods into account.[16] Creon fails to do this because ultimately he is more interested in *his* ruling than he is in ruling well, even if ruling well is restricted to ruling solely for the safety of the polis. Creon's principles reflect perverse priorities and deep misjudgments that bring about the collapse of the polis, a collapse so total that Creon, whose name means "ruler," would have nothing whatsoever left to rule. This confirms Haemon's bitter advice to his father that he should "go be ruler of a desert, all alone. You'd do it well" (739). Rule by edict alone cannot be justified, not even in its own terms. If rule by edict succeeds, it does so only contingently, by framing edicts that happen to accord with broader considerations than any royal right to fiat.

In this way, and to this extent, Sophocles' *Antigone* presents a devastating internal critique of rigid single-mindedness in the service of the supreme right of a single ruler to govern simply and solely as he sees fit, even if officially he does so for the sake of the safety of the polis. Moreover, this internal critique is driven by the proponent of the principles criticized, Creon himself, despite the many attempts to induce him to reconsider. The implausibility of Creon's key ruling principles is evident from the start in his sincere but narrow-minded innovations. However, precisely how drastic and disastrous are his innovations is far from obvious, even to the audience, and certainly not at all to Creon. Creon's stubbornness serves to draw out those consequences in all their detailed significance, which is finally so horrifying that Creon not only follows the Chorus' instructions to bury Polynices and to disinter Antigone (1100–1), he also recognizes and expressly declares the erroneousness of his own original key ruling principles (1261–72). Creon came to these excruciating insights only because he so thoroughly persisted in carrying out his key ruling principles to the bitter, self-refuting end, guiding all of his thought and action by those principles whenever and wherever a relevant circumstance arose. Sophocles' audience comes to understand the

---

16. Regarding the complexity of the good of the polis, see Pericles' Funeral Oration, recorded in Thucydides (1998) II, 35–46; cf. II, 59–64.

breadth and depth of these issues by witnessing their exhaustive presentation by their prime exponent, Creon.[17]

There are deep affinities between Hegel's phenomenological method and Sophocles' presentation and examination of Creon. Chapter 4 considers some important points about reflection and judgment that play a key role in the content of Sophocles' *Antigone* as well as in a proper consideration of the play by its audience. There we shall see how both of these inform Hegel's phenomenological method, and what Hegel expects us, his readers, to bring to his book so that we can benefit from his method.

---

17. Here a brief word is in order regarding the content of Sophocles' play and its importance to Hegel in his analysis of *Antigone* in the *Phenomenology*. Creon's attempt to rule by edict exhibits precisely the key defect Hegel repeatedly points out about intuitionism, conventionalism, conscience, self-evidence, and pure "positivity"—the idea that something can simply be posited and thus taken for granted without any further justification. Hegel's main point about such views is that they cannot distinguish, nor can they provide any method or criterion for distinguishing, between *being* justified and merely *believing* that one is justified. Consequently, these views are incapable of distinguishing truth from falsehood, or distinguishing justified from unjustified claims. Hence such views can neither provide nor account for epistemic justification. Though the point cannot be discussed here, Hegel thinks the same fault also infects simple appeals to (or declarations of) natural law, e.g., those exhibited by Antigone. See Chapter 4, note 6. For discussion of Hegel's criticism of these kinds of view, see Westphal (1989a, 32–4; 1989b, 135–56; 1993, 241–2).

Four

Philosophical Reflection and Philosophical Method

7. Reflections on Judgment and Reflective Judgment in *Antigone*

7.1 Singling out one major theme and aspect of *Antigone* from the others, as done in Chapter 3, omits a key feature of Sophocles' play. *Antigone* is replete with terms for and discussions of judgment; Aristotle recognized Sophocles' commentary on a "rule-following" model of reasoned judgment.[1] The predominant model of reasoned judgment is that judging a particular case simply involves subsuming it under the relevant principle, from which direct consequences follow by syllogistic inference. These inferences may be deductive, inductive, or abductive; the key to this view is that justification lies in inferences that follow from "first principles" of one sort or another. This model of reasoned judgment in terms of subsumption or, analogously, axiomatic deduction, though pervasive, is deeply flawed (Will 1988, 1997). Nussbaum points out that Sophocles' play encourages careful attention to detail, in particular to many metaphors regarding judgment and training, and to many levels within and interconnections between each of the key incidents. She also points out that Aristotle's model of practical reasoning is based on this kind of carefully reflective judgment, which is rooted in careful examination and appreciation of all relevant details.

Nussbaum finds this built into the very structure of Sophocles' lyrics:

> The lyrics both show us and engender in us a process of reflection and (self-)discovery that works through a persistent attention to and a (re-)interpretation of concrete words, images, incidents. We reflect on an incident not by subsuming it under a general rule, not by assimilating its features to the terms of an elegant scientific procedure, but by burrowing down into the depths of the particular, finding images and connections that will permit us to see it more truly, describe it more richly; by combining this burrowing with a horizontal drawing of connections, so that every horizontal link contributes to the depth of our view of the particular, and every new depth creates new horizontal links. . . . The image of learning expressed in this style, like the picture

---

1. See Napolitano Valditara (2002), esp. §§C and F, and Nussbaum (1986), ch. 3.

of reading required by it, stresses responsiveness and an attention to complexity; it discourages the search for the simple and, above all, for the reductive. It suggests to us that the world of practical choice, like the text, is articulated but never exhausted by reading; that reading must reflect and not obscure this fact, showing that the particular (or: the text) remains there unexhausted, the final arbiter of the correctness of our vision; that correct choice (or: good interpretation) is, first and foremost, a matter of keenness and flexibility of perception, rather than conformity to a set of simplifying [*sic*] principles. . . .

Finally, the Chorus reminds us that good response to a practical situation (or: a text) before us involves not only intellectual appreciation but also, where appropriate, emotional reaction. . . . these elders allow themselves not only to "think on both sides" but also to feel deeply. They allow themselves to form the bonds with their world that are the bases for profound fear and love and grief.[2]

About all this, Nussbaum is surely right. She addresses her comments on practical reasoning to philosophers as well as to general readers. Her comments illuminate philosophical reflection.

However, because she focuses so emphatically on reflection on particulars, Nussbaum's observations tend to obscure the fact that such reflections are the basis for forming and reaching conclusions, such as the elders' ultimate agreement with both Haemon and Antigone (802–6).[3] Nussbaum's selective emphasis favors particularism only because she does not consider very well the role of the appreciation of relevant particulars in developing, formulating, and assessing an adequately reasoned view on the matter at hand. Her observations illuminate philosophical reflection, regardless of whether specifically practical or theoretical (cognitive) issues are considered, and regardless of debates between particularists and universalists. This is because the kind of philosophical reflection she describes is required for sound argumentative reasoning of any kind.

More directly: only the careful, reflective examination and appreciation of details can enable us to assess any particular piece of reasoning we engage in, and to assess the relevance or adequacy of any "first principles" or "first premises" we use in our thought, judgment, and action. Only by examining and considering the particular details of the situation and the implications (direct conclusions as well as broader implications) of a piece of deductive (or inductive or abductive) reasoning can we consider whether that reasoning is invalid or valid, germane or irrelevant.

---

2. Nussbaum (1986, 69–70). The phrase "think on both sides" is Nussbaum's (1986, 69) rendering of the phrase in v. 376.

3. Cf. Nussbaum (1986, 70).

Likewise, we can only assess the soundness of a piece of deductive reasoning, and determine whether it should be used *modus ponens* or *modus tollens,* through careful, reflective consideration of both the principles, premises, and inferences of that reasoning, and the particulars of the circumstance or issue to which that reasoning pertains. Only this kind of careful, thorough reflection can enable us to distinguish unsound from sound arguments, and thereby to identify genuine proofs (see §2.3). This point holds true for both practical and theoretical reasoning; it concerns cognition as well as practice, and it concerns our philosophical reasoning about cognition or practice.[4]

7.2 Unfortunately, Nussbaum misunderstands Hegel, claiming that he sought some simplifying and stable "synthesis" that would (optimistically) reconcile two opposed sides (represented by Antigone and Creon) and thereby avoid and resolve their conflict once and for all.[5] This is a serious misunderstanding, directly at odds with Hegel's fallibilism (see §§10, 11, 12.6, 25, 28).[6] Hegel's phenomenological method is designed to encourage and facilitate precisely this kind of careful reflection on and

---

4. Cf. Westphal (1989a, 78–83). Hegel's emphasis on the importance of the particulars does not reduce his view to "particularism." Like Aristotle, Hegel insists that particular instances and general principles must be assessed conjointly. On Hegel's standards of justification in practical affairs, see Neuhouser (2000), Westphal (2003d). For a comprehensive synopsis of Neuhouser's outstanding study, see Westphal (2002a).

5. Nussbaum (1986, 52, 67, 68).

6. Given her stress on careful detailed reading, it is ironic that Nussbaum's error results from not understanding Hegel's philosophy sufficiently to interpret the passage she quotes within the context of his theory of justification, nor within the context of his social theory (which Hegel had hardly developed by the time he wrote the *Phenomenology*). Nussbaum fails to identify the key issue that Hegel thinks Creon and Antigone represent and so cannot identify what kind of "synthesis" he allegedly sought. The "synthesis" Hegel anticipates in the *Phenomenology* is one between the justice involved in natural law (represented by Antigone) and the justice involved in positive law (represented by Creon). Nowhere does Hegel say or think that there is anything automatic or inherently stable about this synthesis. Rather, this synthesis must be achieved and maintained over historical time (Westphal 1989a, 174–8; 1993). Nussbaum (1986, 81) concludes by citing conventions as a guide to proper moral balancing of competing considerations, without noticing that the inadequacy of unreflective appeal to custom or to edict is precisely the theme highlighted in *Antigone* that provides the central focus of Hegel's reanalysis of this play in the *Phenomenology* in order to highlight the key defect of "immediate" spirit: namely, both Creon's and Antigone's incapacity to justify their principles rationally. See Chapter 3, note 17.

appreciation of relevant detail, by the audience, in connection with the key conceptions of a form of consciousness, the use made of those conceptions by that form of consciousness, and the details of the relevant objects or phenomena made manifest by that usage. This is central to Hegel's fallibilist, pragmatic account of philosophical justification, including his phenomenological method.[7]

Whether it concerns knowledge or action, any substantive philosophical theory requires at least some substantive philosophical premises; "self-evident" truths don't suffice (see §2.4). Hence the crucial questions: Which substantive premises are true? Which can be justified? Can they be justified while avoiding the Five Modes of Agrippa or the Dilemma of the Criterion? They *can* be, *if* self-critical reflection is possible, and *if* we are willing to engage in it seriously and deeply (see Chapter 5). Like the choral lyrics in Attic tragedy, Hegel's phenomenological method aims to encourage, induce, and support our developing self-understanding, which is crucial for understanding the principles that guide our thought and action, the context within which we think and act, and how we can and do integrate relevant competing and complementary considerations in assessing and determining our principles and our use of those principles, both in thought and in action.

In the *Phenomenology*, the relevant self-understanding concerns both knowledge and action, for (Hegel contends) human cognition is ultimately rooted in human action. Only through careful, honest, thorough, and self-critical reflection can we sort apparent from genuine proofs; only through careful, honest, thorough, and self-critical reflection can we sort apparent from genuine forms of knowledge as these are presented, developed, and critically assessed in the course of Hegel's *Phenomenology of Spirit*. Only through such careful critical reflection can we sort warranted from unwarranted, correct from incorrect substantive principles required by any adequate and informative philosophical account—including, indeed especially in, the case of one's own preferred views. Hegel's *Phenomenology* requires careful, reflective, self-critical judgment on the part of its readers, especially when readers' views are represented by one or another form of consciousness examined in Hegel's book.

Though stubborn, Creon came to recognize the error of his principles and their consequent practices. Because philosophical error is rarely so directly life-threatening, philosophers generally don't face such dire, self-generated, crushing counterexamples to their own views. It can happen that philosophers are presented with genuine, even internal proofs of

---

7. Hegel's fallibilist, pragmatic account of justification is summarized in Chapters 5, 6 and §§10.5, 11, and in Westphal (2003a).

crucial defects in their views and yet fail to recognize or accept the critical force of those proofs. This is one reason Hegel distinguishes between the point of view of any form of consciousness and the point of view of his "observing" readers: sometimes forms of consciousness recognize the demise of their "certainty," even in its most sophisticated form, and sometimes they do not; they experience the relevant difficulties but fail to recognize that and how those difficulties provide sufficient grounds to reject their initial principles and to adopt more sophisticated ones. Especially at junctures like these, careful, thorough, self-critical reflection, by and on ourselves (as readers) and on the form of consciousness in question, is crucial for recognizing and assessing the significance of the problems that confront a form of consciousness, which are (purportedly) sufficient grounds to introduce a more sophisticated view represented by a more sophisticated form of consciousness.[8]

The significance of this point can be underscored by noting another striking convergence between Hegel's method and Greek tragedy. Some recent scholarship (Janko 1987, xvi–xx) has developed a powerful account of Aristotle's view of tragic catharsis, which ties it to central features of his moral theory, in particular his concern with developing virtues of character and their role in practical wisdom (*phronesis*). Virtues of character involve coming to have the appropriate kind and degree of emotion in response to the appropriate circumstances. Having such emotional responses contributes both to right action and ultimately to *phronesis* itself. In this regard, tragedy offers us an opportunity to learn about the appropriate circumstances for feeling great pity and fear without undergoing life-threatening ordeals. Such learning includes both having the relevant emotions and *recognizing* the relevant situations in which to feel those emotions. Experiencing tragic performances can help us learn both of these morally important things, which are at once affective and intellectual.[9] Moreover, these proper affective *cum* intellectual responses are part of properly understanding the significance of points made in a tragedy. Attic poets used the stage to comment on current affairs and to promote or criticize recent events or developments.

In *Antigone,* Creon ultimately rejects his own views on ruling by profoundly reaffirming an Attic form of life:

> I'm afraid it is best to obey the laws,
> Just as tradition has them, all one's life. (1113–4)

---

8. Westphal (1989a, 125–8, 132–9).
9. *Politics* VIII 5.1339a25, 1340a14–25, 1341b32–1342a16; *On Poets* frag. 4.7 (Janko 1987, 61).

Sophocles' audiences would agree deeply with this conclusion. They would do so, not as an abstract principle demonstrated by a philosophical proof, but as a concrete principle of life, now profoundly reaffirmed on the basis of Creon's harrowing attempt to deny it. They would have reaffirmed it not only intellectually but also affectively, attitudinally, and conatively in the very bowels of their living agency. This is a profound form of self-understanding. How articulate or express this self-understanding may be is a further issue—and a central issue to Hegel's philosophy of Occidental cultural history in the *Phenomenology*. Hegel aims to integrate the profound forms of self-understanding and affirmation found in Greek cultural life with explicit, self-conscious articulation of our world (both natural and social) and the self-understanding that characterizes modernity.[10] Only by integrating both of these can we properly, fully, and autonomously undertake genuine commitments: the commitments to the proper principles that guide our thought and action, and so guide productive cognitive inquiry or guide legitimate action and policy in our individual, social, and political lives (see §§13.9, 20).

8. Reflective Judgment in Hegel's Phenomenological Method

8.1 This kind of thorough self-understanding, at once affective and cognitive, emotional and intellectual, this kind of wisdom—at an express, articulate level—is precisely what Hegel aims to encourage, facilitate, and develop in his readers through his internal phenomenological critique of the various forms of consciousness considered in the *Phenomenology*. Hegel of course reaches many results that can be formulated as conclusions of abstract philosophical arguments. However, to treat Hegel's conclusions only at this level would be to treat them as abstract truths about someone or other and only incidentally concerning oneself. This would disavow the much more important issue that Hegel's method addresses: the conclusions he advocates purport to be important truths about *who each of us is as a human being*. Hegel develops his conclusions in the recognition that only if each of us does recognize who we are, only if we truly and deeply understand ourselves, both intellectually and affectively, both cognitively and practically, can we either think or act rightly. Likewise at the theoretical level, only if we achieve this kind of profound self-understanding can we rightly and justifiably sort warranted from unwarranted and true from inaccurate or downright false basic substantive

---

10. See note 6 to this chapter.

philosophical principles and premises regarding either human knowledge or action. Only if we reach this deep, affective, cognitive, and conative level of self-understanding can we autonomously undertake genuine and abiding commitments to guiding our thought and action by genuine, and genuinely justified, principles and practices. In these ways, Hegel takes seriously the full ramifications of the point made earlier (see §§2.3, 7.1) about reasoning from premises. In this regard, Hegel's *Phenomenology* aims at our deep self-understanding no less than does Attic tragedy, if indeed Aristotle's account of catharsis is cogent.[11] These considerations are very important for understanding some basic features of Hegel's account of philosophical justification, which are central to his phenomenological method, as discussed in Chapter 5 (§11).

8.2 Hegel's *Phenomenology* aims to ascertain the character and legitimacy of human knowledge, both theoretical and practical. Doing so includes a large component of self-understanding, of understanding ourselves as cognizant agents. Our actual cognitive and active powers, whatever they turn out to be, along with the gross structures of the world we live in, provide two sets of constraints on the subject matter of Hegel's phenomenological inquiry. Another set of constraints is generated by his concern to provide philosophical justification for his epistemology solely on the basis of internal criticism of opposed views. (Please recall the features of Hegel's method listed in §2.5.) Hegel accepts this stringent requirement because he is very concerned to avoid the twin philosophical sins of dogmatism and question-begging (*petitio principii*), especially about the nature and criteria of philosophical justification. These theoretical constraints are especially important because Hegel's inquiry concerns not first-order questions about our empirical knowledge of this or that particular fact, but second-order questions about our (purported) epistemological knowledge about the character and extent of our empirical

---

11. Ascribing this view to Hegel will surprise those (especially Anglophone) feminists who see in him nothing but a patriarch who denigrates women and disavows affect. Only a brief remark may be made here. Hegel was sexist, but these criticisms rest on a caricature of him as a mad rationalist, a view belied by his accounts of justification and of action. I grant that Hegel does not discuss affect or emotion by name in connection with his method, which he presents so briefly in the Introduction to the *Phenomenology* that it requires extensive explication (Westphal 1989a). However, to understand the aims and significance of his method requires taking the factors highlighted here into account. Integrating intellect and affect is required for integrating intellect and will, which is expressly central to Hegel's theory of action (*Enz.* §§469Z, 471–82; *Rph* §§4Z, 11, 12, 19) and to his critique of Kant's theory of action (Westphal 1991; 1993, 245–6; 1995).

knowledge. At this meta-epistemological level, where we have few if any obvious facts of the matter on the basis of which to assess various theories of empirical knowledge, it is especially difficult to avoid question-begging, dogmatism, vicious circularity, or just downright error.[12] Hegel seeks to show us how we can avoid these problems, and how we can constructively assess competing theories of knowledge, solving the Pyrrhonian Dilemma of the Criterion. Hegel's solution to this Dilemma accounts for the possibility of constructive self-criticism and shows how constructive self-criticism can be used in the meta-epistemological endeavor to assess competing theories of knowledge.

Very briefly, Hegel proposes to present the basic principles of fundamental and competing theories of knowledge, taking each in connection with its preferred examples of empirical knowledge, in the guise of "forms of consciousness." Each "form of consciousness" is informed by a pair of basic conceptions or principles. One concerns the basic character of human empirical knowledge; the other concerns the basic character of the objects of human knowledge. As a form of *consciousness,* it uses this pair of principles to guide its thought and action so as (purportedly) to know various empirical circumstances and to account for its knowledge of them. Because human consciousness has a self-critical structure (regardless of whether we acknowledge it), each form of consciousness is able to assess and revise both its principles and its preferred examples of knowledge.

These considerations and constraints serve to structure the reflections that Hegel seeks to promote and facilitate with his phenomenological method. These constraints also provide a set of determinate criteria for assessing forms of consciousness.[13] For us, Hegel's readers, to learn from his phenomenological examination of the self-critical assessment of forms of consciousness, we must assess his characterization and presentation of each form of consciousness, and we must assess what can and ought to be learned from each form of consciousness, even or especially when that form of consciousness may happen not to learn what it could have learned about the character and scope of human empirical knowledge. This is es-

---

12. Dr. Johnson proposed to refute Berkeley by kicking a stone. As his final reply to all those who mistakenly thought that his immaterialism denied the existence of ordinary objects and events, Berkeley arranged upon his death for his corpse to be displayed publicly and allowed to deteriorate until it became pungently clear that Berkeley recognized the existence of such things as human bodies, along with public places and the bier upon which his corpse lay.

13. For a detailed discussion of these constraints, see Westphal (1989a, 102–12; 1998b, §III).

pecially important when a form of consciousness happens to espouse a version of one's own favored views. Hegel contends that basic theories of knowledge, along with the forms of consciousness that instantiate each of them, can be arranged in a series of increasing sophistication and adequacy (see §§13, 14). This is the source of the narrative or literary structure of Hegel's exposition of forms of consciousness in the *Phenomenology*. This structure, I submit, was fundamentally influenced by his acute insights into some unappreciated features of Attic and especially Sophoclean tragedy. Hegel's philosophical sources do not suffice to account for the dramatic narrative structure of the *Phenomenology*, which is rooted in the self-generated self-criticism of forms of consciousness as exponents of relevant views and principles, nor for the rich self-critical reflections required of his readers to benefit from his presentation of those forms of consciousness.

Chapter 5 presents the basic features of Hegel's solution to the Dilemma of the Criterion and his attendant account of the possibility of self-criticism. These considerations highlight some important points about the role of critical self-reflection in Hegel's fallibilist account of justification. His plea for the importance of critical self-reflection shows his indebtedness to Sophoclean tragedy, especially regarding the audience's proper approach to the play (§§6, 7). Chapter 6 brings out some important features of the narrative structure of Hegel's *Phenomenology* by considering the sequence of forms of consciousness reviewed in his book, along with the key epistemological conclusions that he thinks are justified by each stage in this sequence (§§13, 14).

FIVE

The Basic Features of Hegel's Solution to the Dilemma of the Criterion

9. Rational Justification and the Dilemma of the Criterion

9.1 Enlightenment philosophers conceived of rational justification inferentially, essentially in terms of axiomatic deduction, a model drawn directly from mathematics and logic. The basic idea is that a conclusion can only be justified if it can be inferred (deductively, inductively, or abductively) from some privileged set of first premises. (This is the subsumptive or "rule-following" model criticized by Nussbaum and Will.) This model may suit formal domains such as logic and mathematics. However, the history of philosophical theory of knowledge (including philosophy of science) from Descartes to the present has largely been the history of attempts to fit empirical knowledge into this model, coupled with repeated discoveries of ill fit. The most serious problem has to do with the privileged set of first premises. What justifies them? Self-evidence has been a perennial candidate. However, the wide variety of first premises that have been claimed to be self-evident instead lends credence to Ambrose Bierce's (1958, 123) mordant observation that "self-evident" means "what is evident only to one's self and to nobody else."

9.2 Put more philosophically, the problem facing such "first premises" is the classic skeptical dilemma posed by Sextus Empiricus, the Dilemma of the Criterion. The link between these issues is twofold. On the one hand, "first premises" are used, in effect, as criteria for determining what is and what is not justified. Conversely, questioning the justification of "first premises" raises directly the issue about the criteria for their justification, and the justification of those criteria, whatever they may be. This is Sextus' dilemma:

> [I]n order to decide the dispute which has arisen about the criterion [of truth], we must possess an accepted criterion by which we shall be able to judge the dispute; and in order to possess an accepted criterion, the dispute about the criterion must first be decided. And when the argument thus reduces itself to a form of circular reasoning the discovery of the criterion becomes impracticable, since we do not allow [those who make knowledge claims] to adopt a criterion by assumption, while if they offer to judge the criterion by a criterion we force them to a regress *ad infinitum*. And furthermore, since

demonstration requires a demonstrated criterion, while the criterion requires an approved demonstration, they are forced into circular reasoning.[1]

This dilemma had a pervasive, though often subterranean influence on modern philosophy. Nevertheless, few Enlightenment philosophers confronted it directly, in part because they were transfixed by an axiomatic-deductive account of justification, which they apparently assumed settled the issue about the nature and criteria of justification.

The Dilemma of the Criterion has had a striking career in analytic philosophy. It was included in a classic anthology in theory of knowledge (Nagel and Brandt 1965, 381), but then vanished from such collections until only quite recently, when it once again was included in such an anthology (Moser and vander Nat 1995, 87–8). Very few epistemologists have devoted serious attention to this Dilemma.

9.3 Hegel restated Sextus' Dilemma of the Criterion right in the middle of the Introduction to the *Phenomenology of Spirit*. Concerned with how we could distinguish genuine knowledge (Hegel's philosophical "science") from merely apparent ("phenomenal") knowledge, and speaking of a "standard" rather than a "criterion," Hegel puts the Dilemma in these terms:

> [I]f this presentation [conducted in the *Phenomenology*] is viewed as a description of the way *science* is *related* to *phenomenal* knowledge, and as an *investigation* and critical *examination* into *the reality of knowledge*, it does not seem possible for it even to take place without some presupposition which will serve as the fundamental standard of measurement. For an examination consists in applying an accepted standard and in deciding, on the basis of final agreement or disagreement with the standard, whether what is being tested is correct or incorrect. Thus the standard as such, and science too, were it the standard, is accepted as the essence or the *in itself*. But here, where science will make its first appearance, neither science nor anything else has justified itself as the *essence* or as the *in itself;* and without some such basic principle it seems that an examination cannot take place. (My tr.; PhdG 9:58.12–22/M52)[2]

Hegel developed an extremely sophisticated solution to this Dilemma (see §10). Hegel recognized that responding effectively to the Dilemma of the Criterion requires developing conjoint accounts of constructive *self*-criticism and mutual criticism. These accounts Hegel provides in the

---

1. Sextus Empiricus (1933), vol. 1, bk. 2, ch. 4 §20; cf. bk. 1, ch. 14 §§116–7.
2. I discuss this and other references by Hegel to Sextus Empiricus in Westphal (2000b).

Phenomenology of Spirit. It is striking that only a handful of analytic epistemologists have remarked on the importance of self-criticism, though none of them have provided an account of it, and none have linked this issue to Sextus' Dilemma.

10. Hegel's Analysis of the Self-Critical Structure of Consciousness

10.1 A careful textual analysis (Westphal 1989a, 100–14; 1998b) reveals that Hegel analyzes our consciousness of an object into six main aspects. He distinguishes the object itself from our conception of the object itself. Likewise, he distinguishes between ourselves as actual cognitive subjects in our actual cognitive engagements from our *self-conception* as engaged cognitive subjects. More importantly, Hegel analyzes the content and character of our *experience* of an object, and likewise of our experience of *ourselves* as cognitive subjects, as *resulting* from our use of these conceptions in attempting to know their respective "objects." Consequently, the character and content of our experience of the object results from using our conception of the object in attempting to know the object itself. Likewise, the character and content of our self-experience as cognizant subjects results from using our cognitive self-conception in attempting to know ourselves in our actual cognitive engagements.[3]

Consider this table of six aspects that Hegel distinguishes:

Six Aspects of Our Consciousness of an Object

A. Our conception of the object.	1. Our cognitive self-conception.
B. Our experience of the object.	2. Our cognitive self-experience.
C. The object itself.	3. Our cognitive constitution and engagement themselves.

According to Hegel, our experience of the object (B) is structured *both* through our conception of the object (A) *and* through the object itself (C), which we endeavor to comprehend using that conception (A). Similarly our experience of ourselves as cognizant subjects (2) is structured *both* through our cognitive self-conception (1) *and* our actual cognitive constitution and engagements (3), which we endeavor to comprehend using

---

3. I stress that the character and content of our experience is at issue to avoid the potential misunderstanding that Hegel might take the object merely to cause our experience. In Hegel's view, objects and events in our environs are themselves the intentional objects of our (outer) experience and empirical knowledge.

that conception (1). Hegel's analysis implies directly that, on the one hand, we have no concept-free empirical knowledge or concept-free self-knowledge. (On this point, see §§13.4, 13.5.) On the other hand, neither are we trapped within our "conceptual schemes"! Put positively, our experience of the object (B) can only correspond with the object itself (C) if our *conception* of the object (A) also corresponds with the object itself (C). Likewise, our cognitive self-experience (2) corresponds with our actual cognitive constitution and engagement (3) only if our cognitive self-conception (1) also corresponds with them (3).

Put negatively and critically, insofar as our conception of the object (A), or likewise our cognitive self-conception (1), fails to correspond with their "objects" (C, 3), our theoretical and practical expectations will deviate—often widely—from our actual course of experience. If we pay attention to such deviations, we can detect and correct this lack of correspondence, though only through sustained and pointed attempts to comprehend our "objects" (C, 3) by using our conceptions (A, 1) in our experience of those objects (B, 2). Such attempts can inform us whether and how our conceptions (A, 1) can and must be revised in order to improve their correspondence with their objects (C, 3).

10.2 The nature and role of these experienced discrepancies is both subtle and important. Plainly, Hegel held long before the term was coined that full justification requires the absence of "defeaters," of telling or compelling counterexamples, counterevidence, or counterargument to an epistemology when its principles are scrupulously employed in practice. Plainly, too, Hegel holds that our key conceptions guide and inform, but do not fully or solely determine, the character of our actual cognitive behavior, of our actual cognitive experience, or of the objects we purport to know. This involves an important element of epistemic externalism: our cognitive capacities and abilities (3), like the objects we engage (C) through those capacities and abilities (whatever they may be), are what they are and function as they do even if we misunderstand them.[4] In this way, the actual object we engage with (C), and our actual cognitive capacities by which we engage those objects (3), can manifest themselves in our experience of them (B, 2) and provide information for assessing or revising our lead conceptions or principles of knowledge and its objects (A, 1). Epistemic (justificatory) externalism plays a second role in Hegel's account of constructive self-criticism, because our experience of defeated cognitive expectations, and especially our experience of whatever defeated

---

4. Epistemic "externalism" is the view that at least some factors that concern the justificatory status of a belief or claim are not, or need not be, explicit (or even implicit) objects of someone's awareness (see §§10.5, 12.2, 28).

them, is prima facie justified by the generally reliable functioning of our cognitive capacities and behavior (3) in connection with our purported objects of knowledge (C) (see §12).

The thought that our actual cognitive experience (B, 2) can diverge from our cognitive expectations, which are based on our basic epistemic concepts and principles (A, 1), raises an important issue about how we recognize whatever defeats our expectations. Hegel's view may appear to face a dilemma: If we can only identify epistemic defeaters by using our conceptions—even if we use more than just our leading epistemic conceptions (A, 1)—can there be sufficient critical or justificatory links between our conceptually informed judgments about what happened and what actually happened? On the other hand, if we have sufficient evidence to revise our lead epistemic conceptions (A, 1) on the basis of experienced defeaters, isn't this precisely because those defeaters defy our conceptualizations and exceed their content? Is Hegel's view able to escape conceptual scheme relativity without relapsing into knowledge by acquaintance?

Hegel's view does not confront this dilemma. In avoiding it, his view occupies a middle ground between two important contemporary schools of thought. One account of these defeated cognitive expectations would be based on Davidson's view (1984). In this view, whatever defeated our cognitive expectations would causally occasion various conceptually structured beliefs about the defeater(s). The links between those beliefs and their purported objects would be causal in one direction and semantic in the other, based on Davidson's truth-conditional semantics and "radical interpretation." In this view, the only epistemic grounds or reasons we have to reconsider our lead conceptions of knowledge and its objects would be our *beliefs* about their experienced failure.

A quite different account of these defeated expectations would be based on, for example, the views of Tye (1995, §§4.1, 4.2, 5.2) and Peacocke (1998), who contend that there is a quite specific, though nevertheless general (repeatable), sensory content in our experience that exceeds our conceptual grasp and that provides the intentional character of sensory experience. In this second view, this nonconceptual (though intentional) sensory content would itself be an epistemic ground or reason that justifies revising our lead conceptions of knowledge and its objects. This view denies that all our experience is conceptually structured while purporting to avoid the pitfalls of aconceptual "knowledge by acquaintance."

Hegel's view is neither of these. As mentioned just above, Hegel accounts for the prima facie veridicality of our experience of defeaters, and the prima facie justification of our thoughts about those defeaters, by appeal to a reliabilist view of our neurophysiology of perception and our

SECTION 10

linguistic competence (via training; see §27). Hegel maintains that identifying the occurrence and character of defeaters, of divergences between our cognitive expectations and our cognitive results, requires using conceptions. Hegel has two basic reasons for this. First, he maintains that all empirical conceptions can be defined and acquired only by using a certain set of pure a priori conceptions, including those required to identify and individuate spatiotemporal particulars or their characteristics (see §21). Second, he maintains that identifying the specific character of a defeater requires using specific conceptions of each of its relevant characteristics. When our cognitive expectations are defeated, we may already have a sufficient battery of conceptions to identify the salient features of the defeater. However, we may not; we may need to fashion new conceptions to grasp newly manifest particulars or features thereof. As mentioned, Hegel holds that the fashioning of new empirical conceptions is guided by certain pure a priori conceptions. He further holds that we fashion new empirical conceptions by differentiating the newly recognized characteristic(s) from those already familiar: whether objects or their characteristics are at issue, Hegel holds that their identification requires discrimination, and discrimination requires differentiation from other relevant alternative conceptions (of other relevant objects, events, or their characteristics). Hence our fashioning of new empirical conceptions is itself conceptually informed, even when it is also informed by very specific features of what we sense through our experience. In identifying a newly discovered characteristic of something we experience, we fashion a conception of it, and we do so by drawing on as well as modifying our prior conceptual repertoire. In Hegel's view, the occurrence of the sensed content is relevant to the prima facie justification of our fashioning and using a new conception with which we identify and expressly grasp that sensed state of affairs. This sensed content is also relevant to the semantic content of our new conception (see §15). However, in Hegel's view, the sensed content contributes to the justification of our express, articulate recognition of the sensed state of affairs and its relevance to our lead conceptions of knowledge and its objects, only through our express, conceptually articulated grasp of that sensed state of affairs.[5] (Hegel's integration of internalist and externalist factors in analyzing mental content,

---

5. In this debate between Davidson and Peacocke or Tye, McDowell's (1994, 1998) views are often associated with Davidson's. However, I think McDowell's view is much closer to Hegel's than to either of these alternatives, although McDowell doesn't consider Hegel's Kantian point about the role of pure a priori conceptions in guiding our acquisition and definition of empirical conceptions.

semantics, and justification is complex; it recurs throughout the remainder of this book, esp. §12.)

10.3 The basic aim of Hegel's account of the self-critical structure of consciousness (and hence of forms of consciousness) is to provide a compelling account of philosophical justification in fraught theoretical domains, such as epistemology. To justify the basic principles embedded in an epistemology, and expressed as a form of consciousness' key conceptions of knowledge (1) and of the objects of knowledge (2), those conceptions must correspond with our experience of our objects of knowledge (B) and with our experience of ourselves as engaged, cognizant beings (2) over a sustained and continuing period of use and critical scrutiny. However, this is only one dimension of Hegel's criteria of justification. In addition, our conception of the object (A) and our cognitive self-conception (1) must mutually correspond, in the sense that we conceive of the object (A) in ways that can be known in accord with our cognitive self-conception (1), and our cognitive self-conception (1) must be of a cognitive subject who can know such objects as we conceive them (A). These conceptions must not merely be consistent, but must positively support each other. Likewise, our experience of the object (B) and our cognitive self-experience (2) must positively support each other. Finally, our conception of the object (A) must render our cognitive self-experience (2) intelligible, and our cognitive self-conception (1) must render our experience of the object (B) intelligible. In sum, the four aspects (A, B, 1, 2) must mutually correspond and positively support each other in the sense that they ground or justify each other. However, for reasons given earlier (§10.1), those aspects can only do this insofar as our conceptions, (A, 1) correspond to their objects (C, 3).

The meta-epistemological character of Hegel's inquiry and method must be kept clearly in mind. Hegel's criterion is not designed to work, certainly not as a sufficient criterion of justification, at the first-order level of particular instances of empirical knowledge, whether everyday or scientific. Instead, it is designed to work at the broad, generic level of the critical examination of basic conceptions of human empirical knowledge, where different conceptions (or models) of the objects of empirical knowledge require different conceptions (or models) of empirical knowledge. At this meta-epistemological level, this complex of correspondences is a sufficient criterion of the truth, and hence also the justification, of an epistemology. Due to Hegel's fallibilism (see §§10.5, 11.2, 12.6), however, our use of this sufficient criterion very strongly indicates the truth of the epistemology in question, though it does not entail that it is true. (Entailment is an infallibilist requirement for justification.)

10.4   Consider two brief examples of the kinds of defeated expectations that pertain to Hegel's phenomenological examination of forms of consciousness. The form of consciousness called "sense certainty" espouses aconceptual knowledge by acquaintance of spatiotemporal particulars (objects and events). In employing these principles, however, it finds that it is utterly unable to account for its ability to designate the particulars it knows without admitting the use of conceptions, and so must rescind its principle of aconceptual knowledge. The form of consciousness called "perception" admits predication into its account of empirical knowledge, but holds (in effect) that observation terms suffice for empirical knowledge of spatiotemporal particulars. In employing these principles, however, it finds that perception alone cannot determine that the white, cubical, and sour properties it senses all belong to the same grain of salt. Thus it must grant that there is more to our conceptual resources than observation terms. (The full series of forms of consciousness considered in the *Phenomenology* is summarized in §§13, 14.) By making previously unaccounted or unrecognized features of the world or of knowledge manifest in such ways, defeated expectations supply information that can be used to revise conceptions of the world and of knowledge.[6]

In this way, we can self-critically assess the most basic principles of a theory of knowledge on its own terms, whether that theory is espoused by ourselves or by others. If we exercise our capacities for self-critical assessment thoroughly and persistently, we do not confront the options apparently forced upon us by the Dilemma of the Criterion: infinite regress, vicious circularity, dogmatism, or question-begging. Circularity is vicious only when it involves nothing but repetition. Self-criticism allows us to reassess and if need be revise faulty members of the series of grounds of justification, or faulty links among them—especially when self-criticism is supplemented by constructive mutual criticism. The problem with standard coherence theories (i.e., the apparent lack of external input) is avoided by Hegel's externalism about justification, mental content, and semantic meaning. However, avoiding the snares of the Dilemma of the Criterion requires full exercise of mature judgment (see §§8, 11).

10.5   Hegel's criterion of justification directly entails a fallibilist account of justification. According to fallibilism, sufficient justification for knowledge strongly indicates the truth of the claim or belief in question,

---

6. I regret the brevity of this summary, for which brief expansion is no remedy. Sufficient details of Hegel's account of forms of consciousness and self-criticism are given in Westphal (1998b); the two examples mentioned are treated in detail in Westphal (2000a) and (1998a).

though it does not entail the truth of that claim or belief. Many philosophers reject fallibilism as incoherent, because if justification does not entail that the truth condition for knowledge is satisfied, then the claim or belief in question may not count as knowledge at all because the truth condition may not be satisfied. This objection rests on an infallibilist preconception about justification. Any sober fallibilist account of justification requires that the truth condition of knowledge *is* satisfied, even if sufficient (fallibilist) justification does not entail that this condition is satisfied. Fallibilist criteria of justification indicate truth—Hegel's fallibilist criteria for the truth of philosophical theories very strongly indicate truth—even though they do not entail it. In this way, fallibilism requires an element of externalism about justification, namely, that the truth condition for knowledge is fulfilled, even if our full justification does not entail that that is the case.

Hegel's fallibilism is based on two main considerations. First, in Hegel's view a philosophical theory of knowledge can only be justified through pointed, prior as well as ongoing and future attempts to use its main conceptions in connection with their "objects" to account for human empirical knowledge. (This is a key point of classical American Pragmatism, to which I return in §11.2.) Second, central to Hegel's account of "determinate negation" is his thesis that a theory of knowledge (like any other philosophical theory) can only be justified through a thorough, strictly internal critique of alternative theories of knowledge. However, the alternative theories of knowledge form no closed series.[7] Since Hegel published the *Phenomenology* in 1807, a wide range of new theories of knowledge have been developed, along with new variants of older theories of knowledge. All of these must be carefully considered in order to reassess and so far as possible preserve, improve, or if need be diminish the justification

---

7. This fact may appear incompatible with Hegel's view that the series of forms of consciousness considered in the *Phenomenology* reaches closure. This conflict is merely apparent (Westphal 1989a, 138–9). Hegel's phenomenological method aspires to closure regarding the general structure of the most basic features of human knowledge. In part this anticipated closure is underwritten by Hegel's confidence that the relevant features of human knowledge are few enough in number to be exhaustively assayed, and that they are not so obscure as to have gone unnoticed during the history of human knowledge and our commonsense and philosophical reflections on it. This level of closure permits enormous range for working out the specifics much more thoroughly. More generally, Hegel aspires to complete his system of philosophy due to his optimism that all the relevant materials are available. The most important point here is that Hegel's claims to closure do *not* follow from his fallibilist account of justification as such. The ways in which and the extent to which Hegel's system is "closed" have been greatly exaggerated and poorly understood (see Kolb 1991).

of an epistemology, whether Hegel's or any other. (This point is discussed further in §25.)

Plainly, Hegel's epistemology and its attendant meta-epistemology require of us *lots* of intensive homework. No doubt this is one reason why philosophers have sought simpler, more straightforward theories of knowledge. Philosophers, especially epistemologists, are often fixated by Ockham's razor.[8] If we seek the truth, we should instead take to heart Einstein's brilliant revision: "Everything should be made as simple as possible—but not any simpler."[9] Simplicity is no substitute for adequacy.

11. Mature Judgment, Fallibilism, and Pragmatic Rationality

11.1 Part of Hegel's account of rationality in terms of constructive self- and mutual criticism can be explained by considering reason in terms of what I have come to call mature judgment. Mature judgment involves the kinds of sensitive reflection discussed earlier (§8). More specifically, mature judgment involves the following abilities:

to discern and define the basic parameters of a problem;

to distinguish relevant from irrelevant and more relevant from less relevant considerations bearing on a problem;

to recognize and to formulate important questions and subquestions that must be answered in order to resolve a problem;

to determine proper lines of inquiry to answer those questions;

to identify historical or social factors that lead people—including ourselves—to formulate questions or answers in particular ways;

to think critically about the formulation or reformulation of the issues;

to consider carefully the evidence or arguments for and against proposed solutions;

to accommodate as well as possible the competing considerations bearing on the issue;

through these reflections and inquiries to resolve a problem; and ultimately,

---

8. This was formulated in the nineteenth century by William Hamilton in its now familiar version, "Do not multiply entities beyond necessity."
9. Einstein (2000, 314). Einstein's editor regards the attribution to Einstein as "probable," though its authenticity remains undemonstrated.

to organize and to present these considerations clearly and comprehensively to all interested parties.

These qualities of judgment are cardinal intellectual virtues. They are central to intellectual inquiry, both theoretical and practical; they are crucial to philosophy; and they are central to any intelligent inquiry in any of life's many activities, whether professional, commercial, political, or personal.

The qualities of mature judgment just indicated are intended as an explication of "mature judgment." They provide no new theory of judgment or of maturity; they clarify by specifying what is involved in mature judgment and by reminding us of our capacity for and frequent, commonsense use of these abilities. Their philosophical importance is revealed by how much more realistic a picture they provide of our actual cognitive predicament, which is not at all dire in the ways that simple logical models of viciously circular reasoning too forcefully suggest. When we retrace or reconsider any complex line (or network) of reasoning, we are not at all condemned to simply reiterating it, and to either accepting or rejecting it as a whole. On the contrary, we are able, often quite easily, though sometimes only with great effort and research, to reconsider each premise, each piece of evidence, and each link in the justificatory line or web of reasoning, so that we can assess the reasoning at hand, both locally and, ultimately, globally as well. The classical skeptical trope of circularity often is just that: a trope, not an accurate or realistic model of actual reasoning. This is not to say that people, especially philosophers, never succumb to vicious circularity; it is only to insist that this plight is far less common, and far more easily avoided, than the logical fallacy itself, and those who wield it as an objection, too often suggest.

11.2   Some of the great significance of mature judgment can be recognized if we bring it to bear on the Dilemma of the Criterion and the question raised earlier about the status of the first premises within an inferentialist account of justification. Any purely inferentialist (subsumptive, rule-following) account of justification inevitably confronts the Dilemma of the Criterion but provides no resources for resolving it, simply because it considers justification solely in terms of inference from some higher, broader "first" premise or principle. Hence this model has nothing to offer regarding the justification of first premises or principles. Either it generates an infinite regress, or a dogmatic assumption, or question-begging (*petitio principii*), or viciously circularity—precisely the fate that Sextus forecast. It is not too much to say that the kinds of relativism propounded by Kuhn, Feyerabend, Goodman, Richard Rorty, antirealist sociologists of knowledge, and indeed by the logical positivists' logical positivist, Carnap, all stem directly from the inadequacies of the axiomatic-deductive account of justification that was central to analytic philosophy of science (cf. Westphal 1989a, 62–4).

However, if rationality is conceived in terms of constructive self- and mutual criticism, in which deductive reasoning has a central though not exclusive role to play, then it is possible to develop a pragmatic account of rational justification. Hegel was the original pragmatist, and the lessons reviewed here were learned well by Peirce, Dewey, and James, however hard they sometimes made it for their leaders to see these important points.

Consider a characterization of pragmatism from Wilfrid Sellars, who notes that pragmatism is a distinct alternative to the two standard accounts of justification, foundationalism and coherentism. Within theory of justification, "foundationalism" holds that some bits of knowledge are basic and are justified independently of any other bits of basic knowledge, while all other knowledge is justified by deriving it from basic bits of knowledge. In contrast, "coherentism" holds that there is no such distinction between basic and derived knowledge, and that any bit of knowledge is only justified by the ways in which, and the extent to which, it coheres with the rest of our knowledge. Foundationalism adheres to the axiomatic-deductive model of justification (even if recent versions of foundationalism dispense with deductive basing relations); coherentism does not. However, coherentism, including its popular recent variant, "reflective equilibrium," cannot account for improvement in the veracity ("truth content") of systems of belief. Standard coherentist views ultimately boil down to just muddling through (see §37).

Sellars comments:

> *Above all,* the [foundationalist] picture is misleading because of its static character. One seems forced to choose between the [foundationalist] picture of an elephant which rests on a tortoise (What supports the tortoise?) and the [coherentist] picture of a great Hegelian serpent of knowledge with its tail in its mouth (Where does it begin?). Neither will do. For empirical knowledge, like its sophisticated extension, science, is rational, not because it has a foundation but because it is a self-correcting enterprise which can put any claim in jeopardy, though not *all* at once. (Sellars 1963a, 170)

Clearly Hegel was no foundationalist. Despite widespread opinion to the contrary, he was no coherentist in any standard (and untenable) sense of the term.

Hegel and his pragmatist successors are all fallibilists; they recognize that human knowledge is corrigible, though they recognize that this is not a curse but instead a blessing. It is a blessing because whatever we may take as first premises, either in empirical knowledge or in guiding action, is justified only to the extent that those premises or principles are demonstrably superior to their alternatives, whether historical or contemporary, that they are adequate to their intended domains, *and* that they continue to perform their roles adequately in the face of renewed occasions of their use, often in changed circumstances. By scrutinizing their functioning in new circumstances and in view of all known alternatives, we can assess their adequacy and we can determine in what regards our principles— even our first principles—and their use require refinement, extension, revision, or even replacement. If we exercise our individual and collective capacities for self-criticism constructively, then we are not trapped in the forced options represented by Sextus' Dilemma of the Criterion and by the regress argument. Circularity need not be vicious, so long as reexamining the relevant network of grounds of justification involves self-critical scrutiny, which enables us to assess, revise, or replace defective grounds or justificatory links within that network. Working principles against practices, working principles against the facts we encounter, and vice versa will appear hopelessly ineffective or even viciously circular to many philosophers. So it must appear until the possibility and the great prospects of constructive self- and mutual criticism are appreciated, and the severe limits of both inferentialist and standard "coherentist" models of justification are faced squarely. It is unfortunate that these crucial points have been so widely neglected by philosophers, even today.

Hegel (like his pragmatist successors) developed a very sophisticated account of meaning in terms of use, well before Wittgenstein gave currency to the phrase. Precisely because the legitimacy and the very meaning of supposed "first premises" lie in their use, they are not static *ideés fixes*. They are instead open to critical appraisal and revision when they are monitored in their actual use. Only through monitoring their use— that is, monitoring *our own* use of them—can we critically assess our own "first premises." This is one key element of constructive self-criticism. Clearly, and especially in Hegel's view, constructive self-criticism and mutual criticism require careful and thorough exercise of mature judgment. Mature judgment is crucial to rational justification. This is one lesson Hegel hopes to instill in his readers through their reflective "observation" of the principles, performance, and pros and cons of forms of consciousness, both individually and as a collective series. With these methodological points in hand, we may now consider some of the substantive features of Hegel's epistemology and the series of forms of consciousness he considers in the *Phenomenology*.

SIX

Some Key Points of Hegel's Epistemology

Hegel's epistemology is so unusual, and so widely misunderstood, that I review it in four stages. First I provide a synoptic overview of his epistemology (§12). Then I highlight Hegel's key epistemological theses and arguments in the *Phenomenology of Spirit* (§13). In a chart I then list Hegel's Table of Contents for the *Phenomenology* and, on the facing page, the key epistemological theses Hegel argues for in each chapter or section of his book (§14). Finally, I summarize Hegel's key transcendental argument for realism (*sans phrase*), and note how it supports Hegel's externalism about mental content (§15).

12. Key Theses of Hegel's Epistemology

12.1 Hegel was the first epistemologist to realize that a socially and historically based epistemology is consistent with realism.[1] His epistemology is nonfoundationalist; he rejects nonconceptual knowledge and the infallibilist ideal of certainty, especially for alleged "elementary" beliefs or experiences. He holds a correspondence analysis of truth (§10.1), though not a correspondence criterion of truth, and he defends a fallibilist account of justification (see §§10.5, 11).

12.2 Hegel's theory of justification contains externalist, internalist, coherentist, and contextualist elements. This is a complex mix, to which I return repeatedly. Note for now that Hegel recognizes that some prima facie justification is provided by percepts and beliefs being generated reliably by our interaction with our environment. Hegel contends that full justification additionally requires a self-conscious, reflective comprehension of one's beliefs and experiences that integrates them into a systematic conceptual scheme (the principles of which Hegel outlined in his *Logic*) that is coherent, comprehensive, and reflexively self-consistent.

12.3 Rationalist elements appear in Hegel's epistemology in his theses that knowledge of particulars requires identifying them conceptually, that observation terms and formal logic are insufficient for empirical knowledge (see §21), and that statements of laws of nature are conceptual

---

1. See Westphal (2003a) for a more sophisticated overview of Hegel's epistemology, focused on his manifold response to various forms of skepticism in the *Phenomenology*.

constructs that express actual structures of nature (see §12.5). He also holds the rationalist ideal that everything worth knowing is rationally comprehensible.

12.4 Naturalist elements appear in Hegel's epistemology in his theses that biological needs (one root of consciousness) involve elementary classification of objects, that the contents of conscious awareness derive from a public world, and that classificatory thought presupposes natural structures in the world (see §15). Hegel's philosophy of mind is deeply functionalist (deVries 1988, 1991); Hegel rejects mind/body dualism (Wolff 1992), though without adopting eliminativist materialism.

Furthermore, Hegel insists that philosophy is grounded in the empirical sciences:

> Not only must philosophy correspond to the experience of nature; in its *formation* and in its *development,* philosophic science presupposes and is conditioned by empirical physics. (*Enz.* §246R)

The importance of this statement cannot be overemphasized. It belies the still widespread view of Hegel as a mad rationalist. Hegel had a model of that mad rationalism, namely Schelling, in direct view, and he learned the errors of those ways early in his career (Westphal 2002b).[2] In his *Philosophy of Nature* Hegel purports to develop a systematically integrated sequence of the basic concepts, categories, and principles developed in the empirical natural sciences, and he claims that this sequence has a "necessity" that cannot be empirically based. I hold no brief, certainly not here, for such a project in philosophy of nature. It is, however, important to note Hegel's clear recognition, in this same passage (*Enz.* §246R), that his philosophy of nature requires that its categories and principles be instantiated by natural phenomena, and that lacking such instantiation would undermine the content and justification of any such philosophy of nature.

This last point also indicates Hegel's rejection of "naturalism" in one of its currently popular senses in epistemology, that the only genuine epis-

---

2. In this very remark Hegel goes on to repudiate in no uncertain terms Schelling's brand of *Naturphilosophie:* "Even less are we permitted to call upon what is called *intuition* and which serves as nothing other than a procedure of representation [*Vorstellung*] and imagination (also phantasmagoria [*Phantasterei*]) about *analogies,* which can be haphazard or more significant, and can only externally impose determinations and schemata onto objects" (*Enz.* §246R). Hegel's characterization of this fantastic procedure fits Schelling's expositions perfectly; e.g., Schelling (1800). One basic flaw in Schelling's procedure is that he conflates analogies with identities (cf. Ferrini 2004).

temic justification is natural-scientific justification. Hegel certainly accepts natural-scientific justification within scientific knowledge, while maintaining that other forms of justification are available in other domains of knowledge, and especially in philosophy. Plainly, natural-scientific justification does not play a role in the account provided here of Hegel's theory of philosophical justification in the *Phenomenology of Spirit*.

Those familiar with Hegel's thought may wonder how Hegel can be an epistemological realist, given his view that reason is "in" nature. The answer is simple: his claim that "reason is in nature" expresses his contention that natural phenomena exhibit lawlike regularities, and that these regularities can be systematized (see §15). So far as reason is somehow teleological, this feature of reason also pertains, in Hegel's deeply functionalist view, to human behavior (deVries 1991) and hence to social phenomena (*Rph* §189 and R) and to human history (Harris 1997).

12.5 Realism in epistemology requires two things: that there be things whose characteristics do not depend upon our thoughts or language (typically, and in Hegel's view, things like human bodies and nature) and that those things be knowable; it requires that there be no cognitively opaque distinction between appearance and reality. Hegel's "idealism" is just such a realism; it is a kind of ontological holism (Westphal 1989a, 140–8; "holism" is discussed in §34). According to Hegel, the causal characteristics of things are essential to their identity conditions, and the individual properties of things obtain only as members of contrastive sets of properties.[3] Hence the causal interdependence of spatiotemporal particulars, along with the constitutive similarities and differences among their properties, establish the mutual interdependence of their identity conditions. This has two important implications. First, particulars have their ground in the whole world-system, because their characteristics obtain only in and through contrast with opposed characteristics of other things, and because they are generated and corrupted through their causal interaction with other things.

Second, Hegel analyzes "the concept" (*der Begriff*) as an ontological structure, like a law of nature rather than a conception, though when we are thinking rightly, "the concept" (in Hegel's ontological sense) is an object of human thought (via the right use of our conceptions). In part, Hegel's "concept" is a principle of the constitution of characteristics

---

3. Brandom (1999, 174) recognizes the centrality of contrastive differentiation to Hegel's account of the determinate content of conceptions and judgments but wrongly labels this with Hegel's term "determinate negation." Instead, Hegel's "determinate negation" concerns the role that internal criticism of alternative views plays in the justification of a philosophical theory (see §§10.5, 25).

through contrast; it exists only in and as the interconnection of things and their properties in the world. Philosophically, we can consider this "concept" in abstraction from the world; this is the ultimate task of his *Logic*. Hegel's "idea" is the instantiation of this conceptual structure by worldly things and phenomena, analyzed in his *Philosophy of Nature* and *Realphilosophie,* including both history and politics. Hegel describes particular things as "*ideal*" because they are not individually self-sufficient, and thus not ultimately real. (Dependence on human minds is thus only one species of dependence on something else, though this species of dependence is not at all central to Hegel's ontology.) Hegel characterizes the world-system as "spirit" because he believes it has a normative *telos* toward which it develops historically. Part of this *telos* is self-knowledge, which the world-system gains through human knowledge of the world.

12.6 Hegel contends that the corrigibility of conceptual categories is a social and historical phenomenon. Our partial ignorance about the world, like our partial ignorance about empirical knowledge, can be revealed and corrected because one and the same claim or principle can be used, asserted, and assessed by different people in the same context or by the same person in different contexts. Hegel's theory of justification requires that an account be shown to be adequate to its domain and to be superior to its historical and contemporaneous alternatives. In this regard, Hegel is a fallibilist; justification is provisional and ineluctably social, historical, and contextual, since it necessarily occurs against the background of less adequate alternative views (see §§10, 11, 25).

12.7 The skeptical view that things are the unsensed causes of sensory experience has been popular from Protagoras to Putnam (c. 1981); it appears in Locke's "thing I know not what" and in one sense of Kant's unknowable "thing in itself."[4] Hegel's analysis of forces and scientific laws responds to this view and provides support for his holistic ontology. Hegel objects to the hypothetico-deductive model of explanation in ways that only recently have become commonplace (Westphal 1997b). He defends a "phenomenological" account of laws of nature. (The sense of this term is distinct from that of his "phenomenological" method.) According to such an account, laws of nature are relations among manifest phenomena (by which Hegel understood natural phenomena, not sense data). This view was prominent throughout the nineteenth century in German and British physics. Hegel purports to show that nothing more can be attributed to any force or set of forces than precisely the array of manifest

---

4. Putnam (1977), 125, 127, 133; (1980), 475–6; (1981), chs. 1, 3, esp. pp. 60–3; cf. Locke (1975), 95, 544–5; Kant, A251; Sextus Empiricus, *PH* I §87, II §§72–3; Plato, *Theaetetus* 182; Quine (1969), 83, 84, 155.

phenomena that they are postulated to explain, so that ultimately there is nothing more to "forces" than the structural interrelation of manifest phenomena. These interrelations are, in Hegel's view, objective features of those phenomena, and the aim of conceiving those phenomena is to formulate those interrelations accurately. Because the interrelations among and within natural phenomena are not known by perception alone, but nonetheless are objective features of those phenomena, those interrelations are conceptual and concepts are structures of nature.[5]

Note that the "concepts" that are structures of nature do not originate in human minds. Hegel distinguishes "objective" and "subjective" concepts. As noted earlier (§2.2), we can clearly keep his distinction in view by distinguishing "concepts," as objective structures, from "conceptions," as conceptual representations by which we grasp those objective structures and the particulars that instantiate them.

12.8 Hegel develops various aspects of his epistemology in different parts of his philosophical system. I detail Hegel's key epistemological theses and arguments in the *Phenomenology* in §§13, 14. First note that his "System of Philosophical Science," comprising his *Logic, Philosophy of Nature,* and *Philosophy of Spirit,* takes up a wide range of substantive epistemological issues. The *Logic* examines the ontological and cognitive roles of ontological categories (e.g., being, existence, quantity, essence, appearance, relation, thing, cause) and principles of logic (e.g., identity, excluded middle, noncontradiction). His *Logic* also analyzes syllogism, judgment, and principles of scientific explanation (mechanical, chemical, and organic or teleological functions) in accordance with which we are able to know the world.[6] The *Philosophy of Nature* systematizes these principles in connection with a wide range of examples drawn from the sciences of his day, about which Hegel was well informed.

12.9 Hegel's philosophical psychology is deeply naturalist and draws heavily from Aristotle. Part One of his *Philosophy of Spirit,* the "Philosophy of Subjective Spirit," treats psychological topics pertinent to epistemology, including sensibility, feeling, and habit under the heading "anthropology"; the conscious phenomena of sense perception, intellect,

---

5. Because misinformation never dies easily, please note that Hegel's notorious views on the number of planets are not what they have been widely taken to be (see Beaumont 1954); they also antedate his mature epistemology. On Hegel's *De orbitis,* see Ferrini (1995). On Hegel's criticism of Newton, see Ferrini (1994), Nasti De Vincentis (1997).

6. The epistemological aspects of Hegel's *Logic* are highlighted by Hartnack (1998) and Stekeler-Weithofer (1992). His functionalism is highlighted by deVries (1991).

and desire under the heading "phenomenology"; and theoretical intelligence, including intuition, representation, memory, imagination, and thought, under the heading "psychology."[7] In epistemology, as elsewhere, Hegel was not only synoptic, he was also thorough and comprehensive.

13. Hegel's Key Epistemological Arguments in the *Phenomenology*

13.1 In the *Phenomenology* (designated by *PhdG*), Hegel argues for some of his key epistemic views in the following ways. To clarify my brief sketch, I provide a chart (§14) that gives Hegel's Table of Contents and, facing it, a list of the key epistemological theses for which he argues in each section of the *Phenomenology*. It may be useful to glance at this chart both before and after reading the present summary.

13.2 To focus Hegel's views properly requires reconsidering a strategic dichotomy in analytic epistemology. It is now standard to distinguish between transcendental arguments, which are supposed to be purely conceptual or (broadly) analytic, and naturalistic arguments, which are causal. Treating these as two exclusive and (as responses to skepticism) exhaustive options occludes both Kant's and Hegel's key transcendental arguments. This dichotomy is too direct an heir of Hume's verification empiricism ("relations of ideas" versus "matters of fact"). The broadly analytic transcendental arguments now current in philosophy can at best demonstrate conclusions regarding relations among our beliefs, or relations among bits of linguistic behavior (Westphal 2003c). Kant's aim in developing transcendental arguments was to justify certain synthetic propositions a priori. Kant realized that this requires richer resources than such conceptual analysis can provide (*KdrV* A216–7/B263–5).

The term "naturalism" is highly ambiguous. In contrast to Frege's rejection of "psychologism," taking our actual cognitive processes into philosophical account counts as naturalistic (Kitcher 1992). However, the account into which our actual cognitive processes, and our capacities that guide them, are taken need not be causal. (Indeed, standard idealists can be naturalists in this minimal sense.) One of Kant's key transcendental arguments regresses from the occurrence of unified self-conscious experience to various necessary "transcendental" conditions that make such experience possible (Ameriks 1978). His arguments rely on our reflecting carefully on our basic cognitive capacities and attendant incapacities

---

7. On the epistemology involved in Hegel's philosophy of mind, see deVries (1988). On Hegel's debts to Aristotle, see Ferrarin (2001).

(Westphal 2003c). Our cognitive capacities are logically contingent but nevertheless are constitutive of human cognition.

By critically rejecting Kant's exclusive and exhaustive dichotomy between the a priori and the a posteriori, Hegel was able to extend Kant's regressive, transcendental strategy to show not only what our basic cognitive capacities and incapacities are, but also to show that certain logically contingent, natural as well as social facts must obtain in order for us to have unified self-conscious experience at all.[8] These facts include, Hegel contends, that the world must present us with a recognizable variety and regularity among the contents of what we experience (§15). This thesis is central to Hegel's internal critique of Kant's idealism, and to his transcendental argument for mental-content externalism (see §15; Westphal 2003a, §4). Hegel's argument is transcendental, though it is neither "purely analytic" nor causal.

Positively, Hegel's method for transcendental argumentation *is* his phenomenological method, discussed in the first half of this book. This method enables us, inter alia, to recognize some basic, logically contingent facts about our cognitive capacities (and incapacities) and about our actual, human cognitive processes, and to justify conclusions that include, inter alia, a logically contingent fact about our natural environment as a transcendental condition for the possibility of unified self-conscious human experience.

In this regard, Hookway (1999, 174–6) is quite right that transcendental arguments are designed to show us why and how we need not succumb to skeptical doubts, and that the skeptical predicament is not the human predicament. Transcendental arguments can appeal to skeptics only to the extent that they admit their fallibility and avail themselves of their corrigibility. To suppose that the only response to skepticism worthy of the name must refute skepticism on its own terms *and* to the skeptic's own satisfaction is already to succumb—in advance!—to dubious skeptical presuppositions. (This is a key reason for Hegel's distinguishing three points of view within the *Phenomenology;* cf. §§2.3, 7.2.) To suppose that, if such a refutation is unavailable, we may as well adopt (causal) naturalism in epistemology is to overlook how much we can learn, and how much can be shown about human knowledge, by transcendental arguments, especially as they are developed by Kant or Hegel.

13.3   With these aims and problems in view, Hegel's phenomenological dialectic proceeds by internal criticism, arguing by reductio ad

---

8. Here I briefly summarize the key points of Hegel's epistemology sketched in detail in Westphal (1989a, 149–88). Harris (1997) concurs with these basic points of Hegel's epistemology (see Westphal 1998c, §III).

absurdum against a whole range of views that deny various claims that he seeks to justify. Each of his internal criticisms justifies a positive philosophical result, and Hegel fits these results together carefully to form an extended presentation and defense of his positive epistemology. Even the later chapters of the *Phenomenology,* which focus on social philosophy, articulate and defend crucial aspects of Hegel's social and historical realism in epistemology (see Chapters 9 and 10). [9]

13.4 Hegel begins his epistemological argument, in "Sense Certainty" (*PhdG,* ch. I), by criticizing naive realism internally and arguing on that basis that human knowledge of spatiotemporal particulars requires identifying them by using a priori conceptions of space, spaces, time, times, self, object, and individuation. Hegel further argues that designating the spatiotemporal location of particulars requires delimiting their location by identifying some manifest characteristics of things. Hegel thus refutes both "knowledge by acquaintance" and concept-empiricism, the thesis that every meaningful term in a language is either a logical term, or a term defined by ostending a sensory object, or can be defined by conjoining these two kinds of terms (Westphal 2000a, 2004).[10] Appreciating the philosophical significance of this point requires some care (see §§21–3).

13.5 In "Perception" (*PhdG,* ch. II), Hegel continues his critique of concept-empiricism by arguing that properly conceiving the identity of perceptible things, and actually identifying them as objects of perception, requires combining the strictly numerical conception of identity with a complex conception of a thing with many properties. This conception integrates the two opposed quantitative partial conceptions, unity and plurality. (I say "integrates" because Hegel shows that no mere logical conjunction but rather a biconditional relation holds between these two partial conceptions.) Hegel argues that we cannot even experience or identify commonsense objects or events without cognitive judgments involving this complex a priori conception of their identity (see §22). This opposes the traditional ideal of purely passive reception of things within our experience (Westphal 1998a, 1998d).

13.6 In "Force and Understanding" (*PhdG,* ch. III), Hegel argues for three main conclusions: our identifying perceptible things with multiple

---

9. Please recall, I do not deny that Hegel's *Phenomenology* deals with a wealth of issues; I maintain that in the midst of all that, there is a continuous argument for epistemological realism throughout his book. I provide a much more detailed summary in Westphal (1989a, ch. 11).

10. Regarding concept-empiricism, see Westphal (1989a, 48–50) and Sellars (1989, 195–213). This way of defining concept-empiricism does not require phenomenalism.

properties requires legitimate use of dispositional conceptions; statements of laws of nature can express actual structures of nature (see §12.5); and we human beings can be conscious of objects only if we are self-conscious.[11] In all three of these chapters (comprised in "Consciousness"; *PhdG*, part A), Hegel thus argues that an activist model of cognition is consistent with realism (*sans phrase*) about the objects of knowledge, namely, that neither the objects of knowledge nor their characteristics are created by our thoughts or expressions regarding them.

13.7 In the Introduction to "Self-Consciousness" (*PhdG*, part B=ch. IV), Hegel thus argues (in "The Truth of Self-Certainty") that biological needs involve classification and entail realism about the objects that meet such needs. In "Self-Sufficiency and Non-Selfsufficiency of Self-Consciousness" (*PhdG*, ch. IVA), Hegel argues that the natural world is not constituted at will. This is an important lesson in realism. In "Freedom of Self-Consciousness" (*PhdG*, ch. IVB), Hegel argues against skeptics and other subjectivists that the basic contents of human consciousness are derived from a public world, and that we can be self-conscious only if we are conscious of objects and events in our natural environment (see §15).

13.8 Hegel's arguments up to this point jointly restate and vindicate the conclusion of Kant's "Refutation of Idealism," that human beings can be self-aware only if they are in fact aware of and have at least some empirical knowledge of the natural world in which they live. However, Hegel's argument appeals not at all to Kant's transcendental idealism. Hegel provides a *transcendental* argument for *realism sans phrase* (and not for Kant's metaphysically qualified "empirical realism")! It has been widely believed that Kant's "Refutation of Idealism" stands independently of his transcendental idealism. Although I believe that it can be made to stand independently of transcendental idealism, Kant plainly did not. He argued that only a transcendental idealist can be an empirical realist (A369–72). In introducing his Refutation, Kant insists that "dogmatic idealism," which he ascribed to Berkeley, "is unavoidable if one regards space as a property rightly ascribed to things in themselves," a view of space that Kant claims to have refuted in the "Transcendental Aesthetic" (B274). The directly opposed conclusion of Kant's argument defines his transcendental idealism. Kant's "Refutation of Idealism" appeals, directly and indirectly, to Kant's transcendental analysis of the conditions of cognitive judgment (B277–8; cf. Baum 1986, 145–9), and Kant argued that those conditions of judgment require transcendental idealism (B69–70,

---

11. On the first two claims, see Westphal (1997b).

B274; Gardner 1999, 186–7).[12] Hegel is the first philosopher to reconstruct Kant's "Refutation of Idealism" *sans* transcendental idealism. His views are thus in line with one prominent strand of analytic Kantianism. The remainder of Hegel's epistemological arguments in the *Phenomenology* aim to provide an historical and social account of human knowledge that explains and reinforces this key conclusion, and that replaces Kant's "subjective deduction," his transcendental idealist account of how we are able to make legitimate cognitive judgments about spatiotemporal particulars.

13.9 It is widely held that Hegel begins his social account of human knowledge in "Self-Sufficiency and Non-Selfsufficiency of Self-Consciousness" (*PhdG*, ch. IVA)[13] by arguing transcendentally that individual self-consciousness is possible only on the basis of consciousness of others. If this is correct, then any self-conscious individual knowledge has a profoundly social basis.

In this regard Hegel's analysis appears to anticipate Wittgenstein's "Private Language Argument" and Strawson's argument to show that we can only ascribe "person-predicates" to ourselves if we can apply them to others. Note, however, that Strawson's argument pertains to our linguistic use of predicates, whereas Hegel's argument purportedly establishes transcendentally the necessary conditions of self-consciousness, not merely self-ascription of predicates. Related views are also espoused by Davidson (1989, 193), who shares Hegel's thesis that "there could not be thoughts in one mind if there were no other thoughtful creatures with which the first mind shared a natural world." Davidson's thesis fortunately rests on more than just considerations about belief-ascription; it invokes constitutive conditions of belief involved in language learning,

---

12. I discuss and criticize Kant's arguments on this last count in Westphal (1997a), esp. 169–79).
13. It is very important to put right the standard, profoundly misleading translation of Hegel's main section title. Hegel's main title is "*Selbständigkeit und Unselbständigkeit des Selbstbewußtseins.*" The standard translation is "Independence and Dependence of Self-Consciousness." However, if Hegel had wanted to focus on issues of dependence or independence, he would have use the German terms for these, "*Unabhängigkeit und Abhängigkeit des Selbstbewußtseins.*" I submit that a careful reading of Hegel's discussion shows that his selection of terms was not arbitrary, that indeed the alleged self-sufficiency of self-consciousness, or the failure of self-consciousness to be self-sufficient, is the central point of Hegel's analysis. This central point is occluded by the standard mistranslation.

mental content externalism (see §§15, 19), and Wittgenstein's rejection of private language.[14]

I mention the aim of Hegel's argument cautiously here, because I am now convinced that Hegel does *not* argue in this chapter for his thesis that individual self-consciousness—in the sense of mere awareness that each of us is aware of our spatiotemporal surroundings—requires consciousness of others. Though initially focused on mutual recognition, Hegel's analysis in "Lord and Bondsman" allows this issue to fall by the side, other than to demonstrate that no such mutual recognition is possible between superior and subordinate. The structure of Hegel's text ought to alert us to his intention *not* to prove here that bare individual self-consciousness is possible only on the basis of our consciousness (or recognition) of other self-conscious people. (For convenient reference, I shall call this "the thesis of mutual recognition.") First, it is very hard to imagine how such a portentous thesis as this could be demonstrated in only a few short pages. Second, it is even harder to find an argument in defense of this thesis within the few short pages Hegel devotes to "Lord and Bondsman." Third, Hegel introduces the thesis of mutual recognition as a bald assertion (*PhdG* 9:109.8–9/M111). This should alert us to the fact that he thereby introduces the key thesis, the "certainty" of one of his *opponents,* in order to subject that thesis to internal critique. Here his opponent is Fichte, who upholds two theses: the thesis of mutual recognition and the thesis that individual self-consciousness is completely self-sufficient, in the sense that it suffices to account for the entirety of anyone's conscious experience. Hegel's main critical points in "Lord and Bondsman" are that these two theses are incompatible, and that the second thesis regarding "self-sufficiency" is false. (On this latter point, see Westphal 1989a, 160–2.)

Hegel does espouse the thesis of mutual recognition. What has gone unnoticed, and hence unanalyzed, is the fact that he continues to discuss this issue throughout the *Phenomenology.* After disappearing from "Lord and Bondsman," the issue of mutual recognition (though not the term) first reappears in "Unhappy Consciousness" (*PhdG,* ch. IVB §c). The recognition considered there is a highly asymmetrical, purported recognition of the devoutly religious, individual self-consciousness by the "unchangeable" (God), which is projected by that unhappy devout individual

---

14. Also see Davidson (1991). On Wittgenstein's argument, see the positively brilliant reconstruction by Wright (1986). The best treatments of Hegel's difficult analysis of mutual recognition are Düsing (1986), Williams (1998), and Neuhouser (1986, 1994, 2003); also see Rauch and Sherman (1999).

(*PhdG* 9:122.7–10, 130–1/M126, 137–8). In the *Phenomenology*, Hegel first mentions a genuine case of mutual recognition at the beginning of "Immediate Spirit" (*PhdG*, part BB= ch. VIA §a): the mutual recognition between brother and sister (*PhdG* 9:248.3–9/M275), though theirs is an undeveloped form of mutual recognition. The first fully developed form of mutual recognition in the *Phenomenology* occurs at the end of Hegel's discussion of "Conscience" (*PhdG*, ch. VIC §c), in "Evil and Forgiveness." At this juncture, two moral judges finally recognize that they are equally fallible and equally competent to judge particular matters, and that they require each other's assessment in order to scrutinize and thereby to assess and to justify their own judgment on any particular matter (*PhdG* 9:359–62/M405–9; Westphal 1989a, 183). This result introduces the theme of mature judgment (§11) into the content of the *Phenomenology*.

The self-conscious "I think" that matters to philosophy is central to rational thought and action in any of its guises. Only such a strong sense of "I think" ensures that we are dealing with thoughts and reasoning, not just vocables or rhetoric. Conversely, anyone who can or does engage in philosophical debate or controversy instantiates this strong sense of the term. This "I think" is, as Kant recognized, the "I judge." Kant's analysis aimed to uncover the transcendental conditions that make self-conscious experience humanly possible. Though Hegel shares that concern (see §15), his focus in the *Phenomenology* is primarily on the kind of self-conscious judgment required to understand and to appreciate the point of, for example, Kant's "Refutation of Empirical Idealism." Mature judgment is necessary for basing knowledge on rational analysis, evidence, and argument. Hegel's thesis is that any of us can only *judge*, that is, *critically appraise* rationally if we exercise mature judgment (see §11), and that due to our fallibility, we can only genuinely exercise mature judgment collectively, in a group setting that supplies critical education and critical scrutiny of and for each of us, through which alone we are able to develop, maintain, and improve our own critical acumen. Hegel's justification of this strong thesis is intricate and requires the analyses that stretch from "Self-Consciousness" through to the last chapter, "Absolute Knowing" (*PhdG*, part DD=ch. III). Some of Hegel's reasons in support of this thesis are discussed in §§20, 24, 28, and 35.[15]

---

15. Hegel's treatment of mutual recognition bears comparison with Aristotle's account of friendship, on which see Cooper (1980). Unfortunately, the structure Brandom (1999) ascribes to "mutual recognition" involves granting the authority to determine the meaning of linguistic acts to the audience rather than the speaker or author. This structure fits the social chaos Hegel identifies in "The Animal Kingdom of the Spirit" (*PhdG*, ch. VC §a; Westphal 1989a, 171–4), but not gen-

13.10 In the first part of "Reason" (*PhdG,* part C/AA=ch. V), on the observation of nature, Hegel argues that classificatory thought, which is fundamental to our discursive, human intellect and hence to our empirical knowledge, presupposes natural structures in the world that we must discover. In the remaining subsections of "Observing Reason" (on logic, psychology, physiognomy, and phrenology), Hegel argues that our capacity for classificatory thought is not merely a *natural* phenomenon. In the remaining sections of "Reason," on practical reason, Hegel argues that our capacity for classificatory thought is not merely an *individual* phenomenon. The joint implication of these arguments is that we individual human thinkers are who we are, and have whatever functioning cognitive abilities and resources we do, only through our engagements with our natural *and* social context; each of Hegel's preceding chapters in fact have analyzed different aspects of one concrete social whole within its natural setting. On this basis, Hegel contends that, in principle, there can be no individual human thinker without a natural and social environment.

13.11 Hegel develops this general conclusion in his discussion of "Spirit" (*PhdG,* part BB=ch. VI), his name (here) for the human community. In particular, Hegel analyzes some key features of our social environment that bear on epistemic justification. In the first section of "Spirit," "True Spirit" (*PhdG,* ch. VIA), Hegel analyzes key tensions and interactions between individual reasoning and customary practices. He argues that our classificatory thought is not and cannot be constituted merely by *custom* or by *fiat* (i.e., not simply by convention; see §11 and Chapter 3, note 17, and Chapter 4, note 6). In the second section of "Spirit," "Self-Alienated Spirit" (*PhdG,* ch. VIB), Hegel argues that human classificatory thought is not corrigible on mere a priori grounds; it is corrigible only in the context of sustained inquiry into the relevant objects of knowledge (see Chapter 5). In the final subsection of "Spirit," "Conscience" (*PhdG,*

---

uine mutual recognition, in which speakers and auditors (or authors and readers) share and acknowledge equal critical status. Brandom's (1999, 167, 175) view is much more indebted to the Carnap-Quine debate—and to Sellars and Richard Rorty (see Chapter 9, note 6)—than to the Kant-Hegel debate, in part because Brandom disregards several of Hegel's key views, including his (nonreductive) naturalism and his account of the self-critical structure of consciousness. Brandom also disregards Hegel's transcendental argument for mental content-externalism and epistemological realism (see §15). Brandom (1999, 185, note 25) acknowledges his debt to Hegel, but his debt rests on selectively and creatively misreading Hegel's text; Brandom's views deviate widely from Hegel's (see McDowell 1999). Brandom's (1999, 179–82) appeal to the model of case law is appropriate, but much better use of it is made by Will (1997, chs. 7–9; 1988), whose views are much closer to, and shed much more light on, Hegel's.

ch. VIC, §c), Hegel argues that the corrigibility of our classificatory thought is a *social* phenomenon (see §§13.9, 27). In the two penultimate subsections of "Spirit" (*PhdG,* ch. VIC, §§a, b), Hegel criticizes Kant's moral world view and his moral theory of action (Hoy 1989; Westphal 1991), in part to clear the decks for his arguments in this final subsection.

13.12 In "Religion" (*PhdG,* part CC=ch. VII), Hegel contends that deities are human projections and that the religious (especially Christian) emphasis on our dependence on God and on our communal responsibilities constitutes an important initial, allegorical recognition of the social and historical bases of human classificatory thought and hence of our capacity to know ourselves and the world we live in.[16]

13.13 In Hegel's closing chapter, "Absolute Knowing" (*PhdG,* part DD=ch. VIII), he draws these considerations together to provide express, reflective, conceptual comprehension of the natural, social, and historical bases of our classificatory thought about and comprehension of ourselves and our world. This completes Hegel's articulation and justification of his socio-historically based epistemological realism.

13.14 Although Hegel's *Phenomenology* defends, by reductio ad absurdum of salient alternatives, only the main parameters of a positive epistemology, it nevertheless presents us with an unprecedented—and, with all due respect to Peirce and Sellars, unsurpassed—scope and sophistication of both historical and epistemological analysis. It may seem that many of the basic epistemic and ontological principles Hegel considers in the guise of forms of consciousness are elementary and perhaps outdated because they are too indebted to modern (seventeenth- and eighteenth-century) philosophy. A closer look, however, reveals that those Enlightenment views have profoundly influenced philosophy, including epistemology, down to the present day (see Chapter 8). With a bit of care, those supposedly elementary or old-fashioned ideas and principles can be found in contemporary theories of knowledge. Consequently, Hegel's epistemology retains great contemporary relevance, some of which is discussed in Chapters 7 through 10.[17]

---

16. This assertion is most obviously at odds with standard notions about Hegel's views. Here I gratefully appeal to Harris (1997); our views accord entirely on this point. Contemporary philosophical naturalism is so dominated by reductionism or eliminativism that the phrase "nonreductive naturalism" may appear oxymoronic. These issues are too complex to discuss here; see the excellent discussion by Rouse (2002).

17. The only analytic epistemologist I have found who pays sympathetic attention to Hegel is Dancy (1985, 227–30). Unfortunately, his treatment of Hegel's views is brief and says very little about their substance. Because he omits the kinds

14. Chart of the Structure of Hegel's Epistemological Argument in the *Phenomenology of Spirit*

The chart on the following two pages displays Hegel's Table of Contents on the left and, facing it on the right, the key epistemological theses that he argues for in each section of his text. The logician's abbreviation "*t.s.*" means "to show"; it designates a key claim to be justified.

15. Summary of Hegel's Transcendental Argument for Realism

Hegel's reputation not withstanding, I have repeatedly stressed his realism (*sans phrase*). Here I sketch one of his key arguments for realism. Much of Hegel's epistemology depends upon his radical reinterpretation of Kant's "Refutation of Idealism," to the effect that we human beings can only be self-conscious if we are conscious of various spatiotemporal objects and events in our natural environs. This argument also supports Hegel's crucial argument for mental-content externalism.[18]

Hegel developed one of his key transcendental arguments for realism and for mental-content externalism through a powerful internal critique of Kant's transcendental idealism (Westphal 1989a, 150–3; 1996). Accordingly, summarizing Hegel's argument requires a brief review of some central features of Kant's epistemology and its attendant idealism. A crucial feature of Kant's "formal" idealism is that the matter of experience is given to us *ab extra*. This is itself a transcendental material condition of self-conscious experience (Allison 1983, 250). Kant recognized one other transcendental material condition of self-conscious experience: the "transcendental affinity of the manifold of intuition" (A113–4). Very briefly, this condition notes that any world in which human beings are capable of self-conscious experience is one that provides us with a certain minimal and, to us, recognizable degree of regularity and variety among

---

of points made in this section, he cannot identify connections between Hegel's epistemology and the contemporary analytic issues that interest him. Hegel also plays central if largely symbolic roles in McDowell (1994) and Brandom (1994). Sellars (1963b, 148) characterizes some of "Empiricism and the Philosophy of Mind" as "incipient *Meditations Hegeliènnes*." Although some of his conclusions accord with Hegel's, Sellars' arguments differ greatly from Hegel's. Regrettably, Brandom (1999, 175) disregards their differences.

18. "Mental-content externalism" is the thesis that at least some of the contents of some of our "mental" states can be fully specified only in relation to objects or events in our environment that are "external" to our minds and bodies.

TABLE OF CONTENTS OF HEGEL'S *PHENOMENOLOGY*

A. CONSCIOUSNESS	I.	Sense Certainty: the This and the Meaning	
	II.	Perception: the Thing and Deception	
	III.	Force and Understanding: Appearance and the Supersensible World	
B. SELF-CONSCIOUSNESS	IV.	The Truth of Self-Certainty [Life and Desire]	
	IVA.	Self-Sufficiency and Non-Selfsufficiency of Self-Consciousness; Lord and Bondsman	
	IVB.	Freedom of Self-Consciousness	a. STOICISM b. SKEPTICISM c. UNHAPPY CONSCIOUSNESS
C. (AA.)	V.	Certainty and Truth of Reason	
	VA.	Observing Reason	a. OBSERVATION OF NATURE b. OBSERVATION OF SELF-CONSCIOUSNESS I: LOGIC AND PSYCHOLOGY c. OBSERVATION OF SELF-CONSCIOUSNESS II: PHYSIOGNOMY AND PHRENOLOGY
REASON	VB.	The Self-Actualization of Rational Self-Consciousness	a. PLEASURE AND NECESSITY b. THE LAW OF THE HEART AND THE INSANITY OF CONCEIT c. VIRTUE AND THE WAY OF THE WORLD
	VC.	Individuality that is Real in and for Itself	a. THE ANIMAL KINGDOM OF THE SPIRIT b. LEGISLATIVE REASON c. LAW-TESTING REASON
(BB.)	VI.	Spirit	
	VIA.	True Spirit; Ethics	a. THE ETHICAL WORLD; HUMAN AND DIVINE LAW; MAN AND WOMAN b. ETHICAL ACTION; HUMAN AND DIVINE KNOWLEDGE; GUILT AND FATE c. LEGAL STATUS

[IMMEDIATE] SPIRIT	VIB.	Self-Alienated Spirit; Enculturation [Bildung]	a. THE WORLD OF SELF-ALIENATED SPIRIT
			  i. Enculturation and Its Realm of Actuality
			  ii. Faith and Pure Insight
			b. THE ENLIGHTENMENT
			  i. The Enlightenment's Struggle against Superstition
			  ii. The Truth of the Enlightenment
			c. ABSOLUTE FREEDOM AND THE TERROR

	VIC.	Self-Certain Spirit; Morality	a. THE MORAL WORLD-VIEW b. DISSEMBLANCE c. CONSCIENCE; THE BEAUTIFUL SOUL; EVIL AND ITS FORGIVENESS
(CC.)	VII.	Religion	
	VIIA.	Natural Religion	a. THE "LIGHT-BEING" b. PLANT AND ANIMAL c. THE ARTIFICER
RELIGION	VIIB.	Art-Religion	a. THE ABSTRACT WORK OF ART b. THE LIVING WORK OF ART c. THE SPIRITUAL WORK OF ART
	VIIC.	Manifest Religion	
(DD.) ABSOLUTE KNOWING	VIII.		

HEGEL'S KEY EPISTEMOLOGICAL THESES

t.s.: Our conceptions of "time," "times," "space," "spaces," "I," and "individuation" are pure a priori and are necessary for identifying and knowing any object or event.

t.s.: Observation terms are insufficient for empirical knowledge; our conception of "physical object" is pure a priori and is necessary for identifying and knowing any object or event.

t.s.: 1. Our conception of "cause" is pure a priori and is necessary for identifying and knowing any object or event.
2. Statements of laws of nature are conceptual and express actual structures of nature.
3. Consciousness of objects is possible only if we are self-conscious.

OBJECTIVE

t.s.: Biological needs involve classification and entail realism about objects that meet those needs.

t.s.: The natural world is not constituted at will; a lesson in realism.

DEDUCTION

t.s.: 1. The basic contents of our consciousness derive from a public world.
2. Self-consciousness is possible only if we're conscious of objects.

t.s.: Classificatory thought presupposes natural structures in the world that we must discover.

t.s.: Classificatory, categorial thought is not merely a *natural* phenomenon.

t.s.: Categorial thought is not merely an *individual* phenomenon.

Implicit result: Individual human thinkers are who they are only within a natural and social context. Each of the preceding sections have analyzed different aspects of one concrete social whole.

t.s.: Categorial thought is not constituted merely by *custom* nor by *fiat*.

(Analysis of the interaction and tension between individual reasoning and customary practice.)

t.s.: Categorial thought is not corrigible merely a priori.

(Criticism of Kant's theory of moral action.)

t.s.: The corrigibility of categorial thought is a *social* phenomenon.

SUBJECTIVE DEDUCTION

t.s.: Religion is the initial, allegorical, premature recognition of the social and historical bases of categorial comprehension of the world.

t.s.: Reflective conceptual comprehension of the social and historical bases of categorial comprehension of the world = socio-historically based epistemological realism.

Note: "t.s." means "to show," following which a main conclusion is stated.

the contents of our sensations. In any world lacking this minimum degree of regularity and variety, we could make no judgments, and so could not identify objects or events, and so could not distinguish ourselves from them, and so could not be self-conscious.

This condition (the "transcendental affinity of the manifold of [sensory] intuition") is peculiar because it is both transcendental and formal, and yet neither conceptual nor intuitive but rather material. The transcendental affinity of the manifold of intuition is *transcendental* because it is an a priori necessary condition of the possibility of self-conscious experience. It is *formal* because it concerns the orderliness (or orderability) of the matter or content of sensation. However, ultimately it is satisfied neither by Kant's a priori intuitive conditions of experience, space and time as forms of human intuition, nor by the a priori conceptual conditions of experience, Kant's categories (A80/B106). As Kant twice acknowledges, its satisfaction is due to the "content" or the "object" of experience (A112–3, A653–4/B681–2).

In this connection Kant (A121–3) argues that a complete sensibility and understanding, capable of associating perceptions, does not of itself determine whether any appearances or perceptions it has are in fact associable. If they aren't, there may be fleeting episodes of empirical consciousness (i.e., random sensations), but there could be no integrated, and hence no self-conscious, experience. In part this would be because those irregular sensations would afford no basis for developing empirical conceptions or for using categorial conceptions to judge objects. (There could be no schematism, and hence no use, of Kant's categories in a world of utterly chaotic sensations.[19]) In this regard, the necessity of the associability of the manifold of intuition is a *conditional* necessity, holding between that manifold and any self-conscious human subject. Necessarily, if a human subject is self-consciously aware of an object (or event) via a manifold of sensory intuition, then the content of that manifold is associable. The associability of this content *is* its "affinity." This affinity is transcendental because it is formal, it pertains to the possibility of a priori knowledge, and it is necessary for the possibility of self-conscious experience.

Kant makes the transcendental status of this issue plainest in the following passage, though here he speaks of a "logical law of genera" instead of the "transcendental affinity of the manifold of intuition":

---

19. A "schema," according to Kant, provides the spatial and temporal interpretation of an a priori concept (specifically, a category of judgment), that otherwise lacks spatial and temporal criteria of use. The "schematism" of the categories is the process by which our basic conceptual categories acquire their spatial and temporal interpretations.

If among the appearances offering themselves to us there were such a great a variety—I will not say of form (for they might be similar to one another in that) but of *content,* i.e., regarding the manifoldness of existing beings—that even the most acute human understanding, through comparison of one with another, could not detect the least similarity (a case which can at least be thought), then the logical law of genera would not obtain at all, no concept of a genus, nor any other universal concept, *indeed no understanding at all would obtain,* since the understanding has to do with such concepts. The logical principle of genera therefore presupposes a transcendental [principle of genera] If it is to be applied to nature (by which I here understand only objects that are given to us). According to that [latter] principle, sameness of kind is necessarily presupposed in the manifold of a possible experience (even though we cannot determine its degree a priori), because *without it no empirical concepts and hence no experience would be possible.* (A653–4/B681–2; my tr., emphases added.)

Despite Kant's shift in terminology, it is plain that the condition that satisfies the "logical law of genera" at this fundamental level is the very same as that which satisfies the "transcendental affinity of the manifold of intuition": in the extreme case suggested by Kant, where there are no humanly detectable regularities or variety within the contents of our sensory experience—call it "transcendental chaos"—there could be no human thought, and so no human self-consciousness, at all. Kant establishes this necessary transcendental condition for self-conscious human experience by identifying a key cognitive incapacity of ours: our inability to be self-conscious, even to think, even to generate or employ conceptions, in a world of transcendental chaos. We can recognize Kant's insight only by carefully considering the radically counterfactual case he confronts us with: by recognizing how utterly incapacitating transcendental chaos would be for our own thought, experience, and self-consciousness. This transcendental proof establishes a conditionally necessary constraint on the sensory contents provided to us by the objects we experience.[20] Below a certain (a priori indeterminable) degree of regularity and variety among the content of empirical intuitions, our understanding cannot make judgments; consequently under that condition we cannot be self-conscious. (Above this minimal level of regularity and variety, there is then a reflective issue about the extent to which our experience of the world can be systematized. This level pertains to Peirce's abductive arguments for "generals.")

---

20. Thus transcendental proofs can justify conclusions much stronger than Rorty (1970, 236; 1971) recognizes. He claims that the most that they can show are interrelations among thoughts (but see Westphal 1998e, 2003b, 2003c).

Kant explains the "necessity" of transcendental conditions of possible experience exclusively in terms of the nature and functioning of our cognitive apparatus ineluctably structuring our experience in accord with those conditions.[21] This thesis defines Kant's transcendental idealism. Though he argues that this kind of explanation also holds true of the transcendental affinity of the manifold of intuition, his arguments for this conclusion are all invalid. The reason is the same in each case: if the matter of sensation is given us *a posteriori,* then *ex hypothesi* we cannot generate its content. Consequently, we also can neither generate nor otherwise ensure the regularities, the recognizable similarities and differences, within that content or among that set of given intuitions. The satisfaction of the principle of transcendental affinity by any manifold of intuitions or appearances cannot be generated, injected, or imposed by that subject; in Kant's terms, it cannot be a "transcendentally ideal" condition of possible experience.

Though it takes further analysis to carry the argument through (Westphal 1997a), the upshot of this finding is that Kant's transcendental idealism is subject to internal critique: a sound version of the standard objection to his arguments for transcendental idealism—the so-called "neglected alternative"—can be deduced from his own principles and analysis in the first *Critique.* Hegel recognized this, and realized that this finding provides a genuinely transcendental argument for realism *sans phrase* and (nonreductive) naturalism regarding the objects of human

---

21. Kant states this most directly in the *Prolegomena* (§36): "Even the main principle expounded throughout this section, that the universal laws of nature can be known a priori, leads of itself to the proposition that the highest prescription of laws of nature must lie in ourselves, that is, in our understanding; and that we must not seek the universal laws of nature in nature by means of experience, but conversely must seek nature, regarding its universal conformity to law, merely in the conditions of the possibility of experience which lie in our sensibility and understanding. For how were it otherwise possible to know these laws a priori, since they are not rules of analytic knowledge but are true synthetic extensions of it? Such a necessary correspondence of the principles of possible experience with the laws of the possibility of nature can only proceed from two causes: either these laws are drawn from nature by means of experience, or conversely, nature is derived from the laws of the possibility of experience in general and is utterly one with the latter's strict universal lawfulness. The first [cause] contradicts itself, for the universal laws of nature can and must be known a priori (that is, independently of all experience) and can and must be the foundation of all empirical use of the understanding; therefore only the second [cause] remains" (tr. Beck 1988, 199–200; tr. emended). Cf. B41, A23/B37–8, A26–8/B42–4, A195–6/B240–1, A101–2, A113–4, A121–3, A125–6.

experience: any world in which we human beings can be self-conscious is one that has a natural structure unto itself that provides us with at least a minimum necessary degree of regularity and variety among the contents of our sensations. Hegel recognized this key problem with Kant's idealism several years before writing the *Phenomenology*, by 1801 or 1802 at the latest.[22] This argument justifies epistemological realism, and the claim that we can know at least something about real objects or events (namely, that there are some and that we experience at least some of them).

This transcendental argument for realism supports the semantic externalism involved in Hegel's solution to the Dilemma of the Criterion (see §§10, 19). This is because the basic kind of regularities, both similarities and differences, in the contents of our experience provide the empirical basis for our developing basic classificatory conceptions (sortals), which are necessary for our identifying and having empirical knowledge of any instances of any of those kinds (or sorts) of things. In §27 we shall see that conceiving these sortals also involves a social dimension, both in semantics and in justification, through education, including language acquisition.

I do not expect Hegel's argument, compressed in this summary way, to be persuasive. Properly developed, however, this argument suffices not only to refute Kant's transcendental idealism (Westphal 1997a), but also Carnap's (1950) rejection of realism and Putnam's internal realism (Westphal 1998e, 2003b). It also suffices to augment significantly Wright's (1992) grounds for rejecting minimalism and adopting a correspondence analysis of truth regarding commonsense molar objects and events (Westphal 1998e). Hence Hegel's epistemology has significant implications for contemporary philosophy. I consider several more such implications in the remaining chapters.

---

22. The textual evidence for this must be carefully assembled; see Westphal (1996).

SEVEN

Some Contemporary Points of Relevance of Hegel's Epistemology

16. Realism and the Social and Historical Aspects of Human Knowledge

One prominent point of relevance of Hegel's views to contemporary epistemology lies in his basic contention that epistemological realism is consistent with a social and historical account of human knowledge. This stands in stark contrast to the pervasive assumptions, common from the Enlightenment to the present day, that realism requires an individualist epistemology, and that any social or historical account of human knowledge must reject realism. Now that controversies that occupied Hegel about realism versus historicist relativism have once again returned to the center stage of philosophy, a few analytic epistemologists have finally recognized that this dichotomy is faulty (e.g., Alston 1994; Kitcher 1994; Longino 1994; Solomon 1994a; McDowell 1994; Haack 1998, ch. 6).

17. Cognitive Activity and Realism about the Objects of Human Knowledge

Combining realism with a social and historical account of human knowledge requires addressing several problems. One key problem is the real bone of contention underlying the dogged debate between coherentism and foundationalism. The key underlying issue in this debate is whether an activist epistemology is consistent with commonsense realism. Traditionally, both sides to this debate have assumed, even feared, that they are not; if the mind actively contributes to empirical knowledge, must it not inevitably obscure its intended objects (Stroud 1984, 258)? Hence coherentists have tended (wittingly or not) to be non- or antirealists, while foundationalists have been ardent realists and have accordingly rejected coherentism. The shared, underlying assumption is that realism requires some basic level of cognition that is purely passive, in which recognizing some purported individual state of affairs requires no interpretation of it, no consideration of collateral evidence, nor even mediating conceptions. (Requiring certainty or incorrigibility or infallibility only highlighted, and exacerbated, this more basic demand for conception-free, mutually independent instances of basic knowledge.)[1] Hegel notes, however, that this is a non sequitur. An activist epistemology is consistent with commonsense realism; that much Hegel shows in the "Consciousness" section (*PhdG*, chs. 1–3). The constructivist supposition to the contrary is well put by Lavine:

> The distinguishing feature of interpretationism, from the German Enlightenment through American pragmatism to mid-twentieth century *Wissenssoziologie*, is an affirmation of the activity of mind as a constituent element in the object of knowledge. Common to all of these philosophical movements ... is the epistemological principle that mind does not apprehend an object which is given to it in completed form, but that through its activity of providing an interpretation or conferring meaning or imposing structure, mind in some measure constitutes or "creates" the object known. (Lavine 1949, 526)

Hegel, pragmatic realists (such as Peirce, Dewey, and Will), and now McDowell (1994), contend that empirical knowledge must be interpretive in order to *re*construct, not to create or complete, the object known. Note, too, that because the sought-after "basic" kind of foundational knowledge requires individualism in epistemology, showing that such "basic" knowledge is not required by realism undercuts one ground favoring individualism in epistemology.

18. Justificatory "Coherence" and Realism about the Objects of Human Knowledge

Another key problem involved in reconciling a social and historical account of human knowledge with commonsense realism is to show how a coherentist account of justification can be combined with realism. One step this requires is straightforward: unlike many epistemologists on both sides of this debate, Hegel distinguished between the nature of truth ("correspondence") and the criteria of truth ("coherence")—and he kept this distinction clearly in view.[2]

---

1. See Westphal (1989a, 62–4), where I trace this theme through the writings of Russell, Schlick, Ayer, Hempel, Neurath, Reichenbach, C. I. Lewis, and Waismann. (Please note an emendation to this text: note 121 on page 246 should mention Schlick, not Ayer, and the correct page number in "FK" is 213, not 214.)
2. Both the distinction and the justificatory link between the nature and criteria of truth are centrally embedded in Hegel's solution to the Dilemma of the Criterion (see §10). Moser, Mulder, and Trout (1998, 69) take for granted that Hegel held a coherence theory of truth, though they later (83) acknowledge that some

Another step is more subtle. It is hard, if not impossible, to prevent coherentism from sliding into relativism or at least antirealism if the relevant kind of "coherence" involves only inferential relations among propositions. Almost any consistent set of propositions can contain such propositions as "And this set of sentences is the true one," or "These observation sentences were uttered by scientists of our cultural circle." Realism is jeopardized—if not thwarted—by the semantic ascent, from the material to the formal mode of speech, characteristic of classical analytic philosophy.[3] The formal mode of speech treats philosophical issues only metalinguistically and eschews talk about things and hence our relations to things. Thus the formal mode of speech omits evidentiary or informational relations between persons and the objects or events about which they have beliefs and of which they may have knowledge. Separating propositions from the world in this way results in conceptual scheme relativity (Westphal 1989a, 56–7).

In this regard, it is crucial that Hegel's solution to the Dilemma of the Criterion (see Chapter 5) involves coherence, not just between our conceptions of knowledge and of the world, but also among these and what our knowledge and the world we know are like *for us*. What our knowledge and the world we know are like *for us* is a function of how we use our conceptions of knowledge and of the world to grasp knowledge itself and the world itself.

Part of Hegel's point was well put by Strawson, who noted that our basic conceptions

> enter most intimately and immediately into our common experience of the world. They are what . . . we *experience* the world *as* exemplifying . . . experience is awareness of the world as exemplifying *them*. (Strawson 1974, 14–5)[4]

---

scholars regard him as propounding (only?) a coherence theory of justification. They claim (152–4) that the Dilemma of the Criterion has no settled solution, though they disregard Hegel's response to it.
3. The distinction between the "material" and the "formal" modes of speech was introduced by Carnap (1934). The "material" mode of speech is the ordinary mode. In it, our sentences or statements typically appear to be about extralinguistic entities or events. Carnap held that this mode of speech is misleading in philosophy, because philosophical problems are all linguistic. To keep this clearly in view, Carnap proposed translating philosophically salient statements into the "formal" mode of speech, in which sentences are only about linguistic entities. The "formal" mode of speech is thus metalinguistic and explicitly marks sentences as relative to a particular linguistic framework.
4. Strawson claims that this is a principle of "empiricism," but he does not explain why it is. Empiricism has no monopoly on this thesis.

Hegel's point is that the character and content of our experience—what is *for us*—is a function both of our conceptions and of the objects or events themselves that we grasp with our conceptions. Experience is our access to the world; it is rooted in the world even while it is also conditioned by what conceptions we use and how we use them in grappling with the world, both cognitively and practically. Consequently, Hegel's criterion of justification (of forms of consciousness) *is* rooted in knowledge and the world *themselves,* and yet does not require us to "get outside our conceptual schemes," as it is (too often) said, in order to assess or to justify our accounts of knowledge and the world. In this way, Hegel's criterion of justification avoids the fault of standard "coherence" theories of justification, that the focus on internal coherence of beliefs or propositions disregards if not precludes input from how things are, and so allows our beliefs or propositions to float free of the world we purport to know.

19. Hegel's Semantic Externalism

The reason we don't need to escape our "conceptual schemes" through "knowledge by acquaintance" is that Hegel's brilliant solution to the Dilemma of the Criterion rejects one of the chestnuts of analytic philosophy, namely, the Russellian version of Frege's slogan that "sense determines reference." More specifically, Hegel rejects the idea that semantic reference is solely a matter of the "sense" of an assertion, where that sense (or its content) can be parsed as a description—the so-called "descriptions theory" of reference, including its current assertibilist descendants. Descriptionalist theories of reference are deeply Cartesian, for they maintain the transparency of intended reference. According to such views, we know and must know what we intend to refer to, because we know what our statements mean, because we can parse this meaning as a description (Burge 1979, 102). (This view descends directly from Russell's theory of descriptions.) Although we often do know what we intend to refer to in this way, it is not a necessary truth, and thinking otherwise locks us into a quagmire of conceptual scheming. Note, for example, that the descriptions theory of reference plays a key role in Kuhn's original arguments for paradigm incommensurability and against scientific realism, whence it became standard fare in arguments against realism (Westphal 1989a, 146–8). Though the alleged relativity of conceptual schemes or (in Carnap's terms) linguistic frameworks is supported by excessive semantic holism (Fodor and LePore 1992; Will 1997, 91–6, 141), rescinding such holism does not, by itself, solve the problem of conceptual scheme relativity. Descriptionalist views of reference are a prime source of the seductive but deeply misleading idea that conceptual schemes *have* "insides" and "outsides," and that never the twain shall be known to meet because (supposedly) we're trapped on the "inside." Such views will forever motivate philosophers to chase the phantom of escape via alleged nonconceptual "knowledge by acquaintance."

Here I think Burge's (1979, 73; 1986) original criticisms of "individualism" are, as he recognizes, in league with Hegel. Burge (1979, 92) is right that, although the phenomena that support his criticisms can be forced to fit into the individualist-Cartesian framework, they are not illuminated by so doing. Like Hegel, Burge rejects the core of the descriptionalist theory of reference.[5] Burge's conclusions are quite in line with Hegel's conclusions in "Self-Consciousness" (*PhdG*, part B), which favor an "externalist" account of mental content (see §15). Externalism about mental content is the thesis that many (especially basic) "mental" contents can be specified only by their relations to parts or features of a subject's environment, the world (see §27). Semantic externalism is the related thesis that at least some of the meaning of significant terms or phrases can only be specified by specifying relevant objects or events in the world around us. In this view, meaning and mental content are more than matters of implicit descriptions, and as speakers we can err in significant ways about what we mean or think.

"Knowledge by acquaintance" was supposed to provide a direct tie between mental contents—our thoughts or beliefs—and objective states of affairs. Externalism about mental content fulfills this need without requiring aconceptual knowledge and without raising the strictly irrelevant issues involved in indubitability, infallibility, or incorrigibility. Hegel argues transcendentally for an externalist account of basic mental contents in "Self-Consciousness" and the first section of "Reason," "Observing Reason" (see §15; Westphal 1989a, 160–9; 1996).

Note that Hegel's arguments for mental-content externalism are cast in very broad terms that avoid the problem that Stroud (1999, 169) poses with many such arguments, namely: "Even if our thoughts have content at all only because we are ultimately connected in some ways with something that is actually so in the world, how is it to be established that water in particular must exist if we have thoughts and beliefs about water?" Hegel's argument focuses on the former circumstance and does not require the details involved in the latter clause. (Hegel's approach is closer to Stroud's sketch of the case for color conceptions in the remainder of his paper; see §27.)

---

5. Burge (1979, 83) notes that his key "thought experiment does appear to depend on the possibility of someone's having a propositional attitude despite an incomplete mastery of some notion in its content."

In this connection, I submit that Hegel is right to side with recent critics of descriptions theories of reference (e.g., Donnellan 1966; Kripke 1972; Wettstein 1991). Note too that Hegel's theory of justification shares much with Haack's (1993) "foundherentism," though Hegel emphasizes much more than Haack (1998, ch. 6) the social dimensions of epistemic justification.

20. Reason versus Tradition?

20.1 The Cartesian individualism that supposedly (if erroneously) is required for realism is undergirded by another dichotomy, pervasive since the Enlightenment, that reason and tradition are distinct and independent resources: because tradition is a social phenomenon, reason must be an independent, individualist phenomenon. Otherwise it could not assess or critique tradition, because criticizing tradition requires an independent, "external" standpoint and standards. Conservatives and other traditionalists contended that we have no such independent power of reason; Enlightenment reformers insisted that we do. Hegel contends, rightly, I submit, that this dichotomy and the supposition on which it rests are specious.[6] In a word, the assumption that reason must be independent of tradition in order to assess it ascribes superhuman (sui generis) powers to human reason and disregards the possibility of and prospects for internal criticism, self-criticism, and productive mutual criticism (see Chapter 5 and §13.9).[7]

To be more specific, most of the conceptions in terms of which we formulate and consider our own thoughts are *learned* and inherited from collective commonsense or specialized (technical or scientific) social forms of inquiry (see §§20.2, 27). This is why philosophers of education have taken constructivism (in a broad sense) for granted, at least since Lessing (1780). This point has been discussed by Burge (1979, 1986), who

---

6. On this count, McDowell (1994, 84–5, 98–9, 126, 184–7) and Will (1997, ch. 6) concur with Hegel.

7. Price (1932, 192) and Sellars (1963b, 170) note the importance of self-criticism in empirical knowledge, but they do not examine it or explain its possibility. Quine insists that any statement can be revised, and likewise any can be retained come what may, though he does not consider whether or under what circumstances revision or preservation may be justified, nor indeed how such changes can or should occur, other than as a reassessment of one's acceptance of various propositions. Nothing more than this appears to be involved in his treatment (1953, 42) of the reevaluation of truth-values. Hence Quine only has an account of changing one's mind, not of self-criticism.

points out that in many cases, the contents of individual thoughts (and other propositional attitudes) can only be properly understood by recognizing how individuals rely on social standards of meaning and other intellectual social norms in formulating, assessing, or revising their own propositional attitudes.

The harsh reception of Burge's work by traditional individualists in the philosophy of mind shows how tenacious are the dichotomies identified here. The basic response by individualist philosophers of mind has been to define into existence a "narrow" notion of mental content that includes all and only those aspects of propositional attitudes that are independent of an individual's social and physical environment. This move directly parallels Descartes' definition of sensing in the "strict" sense as whatever he *seems* to perceive (Meditation 2). Unfortunately, under pressure of such criticism, Burge's appeals to speakers' social context have become incidental; ultimately, he uses them only to attack the related Cartesian idea that (to borrow Putnam's phrase) "meaning is in the head." Burge now defines "individualism" in a way that is entirely independent of social ontology:

> Anti-individualism is the view that not all of an individual's mental states and events can be type-identified independently of the nature of the entities in the individual's environment. (Burge 1992, 46–7)

Unfortunately absent is the social cast of Burge (1979).[8]

20.2 The positive point about traditions providing the basis for intelligent thought and action is put well by Green (1999): education is a matter of acquiring norms. The norms we acquire through education run the gamut from norms of grammar and linguistic usage—including all explicit forms of classification—to etiquette, ethics, and methods of intellectual inquiry across the disciplines, including the sciences. As Peirce remarked:

> Every physicist, and every chemist, and, in short, every master of any department of experimental science, has his mind moulded by his life in the laboratory to a degree that is little expected. (1905; *CP* 5 §411)

The same holds for training in any field, including graduate programs, and including those in philosophy. (This is one factor perpetuating the specious dichotomies criticized by Hegel.) This is not to say that the objects of human knowledge in the sciences and other disciplines are human constructs; it is to say instead that the conceptions, principles, techniques,

---

8. Individualism is considered in more detail in Chapter 10.

and procedures of disciplined intellectual inquiry are normative human constructs. When those constructs work well, they do inform us about actual features of the objects investigated. These remarks appear to stress the content of the various norms, principles, and procedures one learns through education, or in mastering a discipline. Equally if not more important, however, are the intellectual skills and abilities to *use* these norms, principles, or procedures *properly:* acquiring the abilities to judge reliably whether, when, or how a norm, principle, or procedure is appropriate to one's task at hand. To acquire and to exercise such abilities is to assume responsibility for one's judgments, by making whatever judgment is best warranted in view of all available relevant considerations. To assume responsibility for making judgments and for making any and every particular judgment—all of which are, per force, one's *own* judgments—is to exercise autonomy in at least two senses. First, judgment is autonomous because one makes one's own judgment, rather than following anyone else's judgment. Second, judgment is autonomous because it is guided by the normative considerations of appropriate evaluation of both evidence and principles of reasoning. If judgment, as a physiological or psychological process is in some way causal, nevertheless it counts as judgment only because it responds to such normative considerations, rather than merely to causal antecedents as such. Judgment is a response to, not merely an effect of, its proper (evidentiary or inferential) antecedents. Correct or justified judgment is a *proper* response to these evidentiary or inferential antecedents (see §11). If justificatory processes turn out to be causal, they are justificatory not because they are causal, but because they satisfy sufficient normative constraints—defining or at least including *proper* functioning—to provide epistemic justification. For this reason, Kant held that reason, that is, rational judgment (a pleonasm), is spontaneous. This merits closer consideration.

20.3   Kant famously emphasized the spontaneity of human thought, and Hegel followed suit. Kant contends that freedom is a rational idea that is constitutive—indeed, definitive—of our conceiving of ourselves as agents (Allison 1997). Only rational spontaneity enables us to appeal to principles of inference and to make rational judgments, both of which are normative because each rational subject considers for him- or herself whether available procedures, evidence, and principles of inference warrant a judgment or conclusion. In the theoretical domain of knowledge, *having* adequate evidence or proof requires *taking* that evidence or proof to be adequate; in the practical domain of deliberation and action, *having* adequate grounds for action requires *taking* those grounds to be adequate (see §11). We *act* only insofar as we take ourselves to have reasons, even in cases of acting on desires, where we must take those desires as appropriate and adequate reasons to act. Otherwise we abdicate rational considerations and absent ourselves from what Sellars calls "the space of reasons" and merely behave. In that case, to borrow McDowell's terms (1994, 13), we provide ourselves with only excuses and exculpations, but not reasons or justifications, for acting or believing as we do.[9]

Kant's conception of rational spontaneity opposes empiricist accounts of beliefs and desires as merely causal products of environmental stimuli, and it opposes empiricist accounts of action, according to which we act on whatever desires are (literally) "strongest." We think and act rationally only insofar as we judge the merits of whatever case is before us.[10] Judging the merits of a case is something each of us must learn to do; a primary goal of education is to facilitate this learning. Many of the most important results of education concern not factual knowledge but the mastery of intellectual skills and abilities, in sum, the mature judgment discussed earlier (§11). These qualities of judgment are cardinal intellectual virtues. These qualities of judgment must be studied, learned, and practiced. They are socially acquired character traits and intellectual skills that are absolutely fundamental to individual autonomy (cf. Pettit 1996; Baier 1997), and they are crucial to the justification and to the justificatory status of our cognitive judgments.

20.4 A hallmark of Hegel's social philosophy and philosophy of history is that our particular communities, and ultimately the human community as a whole, contribute fundamentally to the development of mature individual judgment. For this to happen, we must avail ourselves of, and so far as possible master and critically assess, the achievements of our predecessors, just as Hegel exhorts us to do in his Preface, and as

---

9. Note that I do not claim that taking evidence to be adequate suffices for that evidence to be adequate! Some epistemologists bridle at the notion that having adequate evidence or grounds for belief requires taking that evidence or those grounds to be adequate. Yet there are many examples of people having memories or perceptions that in fact bear evidentially on a certain belief they hold, though they fail to recognize this evidential relation and so fail to base their belief on that evidence. Basing (or, mutatis mutandis, rejecting) beliefs on evidence requires taking that evidence to be both relevant and adequate.

10. This is to say, Kant's account of rational spontaneity generalizes what Allison (1990, 5–6, 39–40) calls Kant's "Incorporation Thesis," that no inclination becomes a motive unless and until it is incorporated into an agent's maxim. Hegel restates Kant's Incorporation Thesis in his own terms in his *Philosophy of Right* (§§5–7), where he also extols Kant's account of autonomy (§135R).

he tries to facilitate our doing in the body of the *Phenomenology*.[11] All this is required for highly informed, philosophically mature judgment. This exalted kind of judgment, however, should not occlude the fact that judgment is required to draw conclusions from premises or to use intellectual principles, whether cognitive or practical. Mature judgment is central to epistemic justification. Mature judgment is socially based, not merely causally, as a matter of education and training, but normatively, in at least two regards. First, the norms and principles involved in any judgment have implications far beyond the present context, and indeed far beyond the purview of any individual (human) judge. Consequently, those norms and principles are subject to the critical scrutiny of others. Indeed, those norms and principles have the content they do and are justified to whatever extent they are, only through their critical scrutiny by all concerned parties, presently, historically, and in the future. Second, due to our fallibility (see §§7.2, 10.2, 11.2, 12.5, 13.9), any particular judgment anyone makes is justified only to the extent that the judge does his or her utmost to exercise mature judgment on that occasion, *and* to the extent that that judgment survives critical scrutiny by all concerned parties. Because mature judgment is socially based, so is epistemic justification.[12] (Hegel's reasons for holding this thesis are considered further in, especially, §§20, 24, 28, and 35.)

Despite its obvious importance, Hegel's account of the social aspects of human knowledge remains essentially unanalyzed.[13] I return to it shortly in Chapters 9 and 10. Before developing these issues further, it is important to consider some relations between Hegel's epistemology and twentieth-century empiricism. This is the task of the next chapter.

---

11. Fortunately, we now have Harris' (1997) magnificent guide to the astounding wealth of material Hegel assimilated in the *Phenomenology*. *Hegel's Ansichten über Erziehung und Unterricht* (Hegel [1853] 1974) contains Hegel's extensive discussions of education.

12. "Judgment" has largely fallen by the wayside in analytic epistemology, except for an innocuous sense of identifying commonsense objects in one's environs. Kant insisted that rules require judgment for their application (A132–4/B171–3). In effect, Wittgenstein's skepticism about rule-following makes the same point, that principles are not algorithms, and indeed that their use requires social training and context (Savigny 1991; Will 1997, chs. 7–9). Elgin (1999) discusses related issues.

13. In this connection, I suggest that Hegelians have much to learn from Will's (1997) pragmatic-realist account of the social nature of norms, including cognitive norms.

EIGHT

Hegel and Twentieth-Century Empiricism

21. Hegel's Justification of (Pure) A Priori Conceptions

21.1 In 1922 Russell declared,

> I should take "back to the 18th century" as a battle-cry, if I could entertain any hope that others would rally to it. (Russell 1994, *CP* 9:39)

His exhortation was unexpectedly effective. For example, it is reflected in Quine's contention that the "Humean predicament is the human predicament" (Quine 1969, 72, cf. 74, 76). Likewise, Simon Blackburn's account in *Ruling Passions* (1998) is guided by confidence in the fundamental soundness of Hume's philosophy. Russell's declaration gave voice to the early hope of analytic philosophers to develop a tenable empiricism built with a sophisticated formal logic. Certainly this was a plausible strategy and well worth trying. However, it didn't work, indeed for reasons that were plain in the modern period. The most sophisticated and adequate version of logical empiricism—Carnap's—fails, and it fails on internal grounds highlighted by Hegel's phenomenological method (Westphal 1989a, 47–67). One problem with logical empiricism concerns its recourse to "knowledge by acquaintance" (Westphal 1989a, 59–60); that move Hegel countered already in "Sense Certainty" (see §13.4).[1] Another problem with logical empiricism concerns its recourse to "concept-empiricism," in the sense specified in §13.4. Hegel criticized concept-empiricism—soundly, I submit—in "Sense Certainty" and in "Perception" (Westphal 2000a, 1998a).

"Concept-empiricism" in the strict sense has been widely repudiated since the late 1950s, though philosophers have not suddenly embraced "a priori" conceptions as a result. To focus Hegel's issue requires distinguishing those conceptions that cannot be defined solely on the basis of concept-empiricism, which we now know to be virtually all conceptions, from a much more limited subset of those conceptions, such as those stressed by Hegel: 'space', 'spaces', 'time', 'times', 'self', 'other', 'individuation', 'physical object', and 'cause'. Even within the recent

---

1. Hegel's arguments in "Sense Certainty" converge in some important regards with those of Evans (1975); see Westphal (2000a, notes 49, 96).

broad rejection of concept-empiricism, these conceptions retain a special status that may be called "pure" a priori. This can be seen by introducing a broader definition of "empirical conception": a conception is "empirical" if we can only acquire it by experiencing particular instances of the relevant kind of object or event, or if it can only be defined by reference to examples of the relevant kind of object or event. These definitions retain the core idea of acquiring conceptions through experience of their instances, while dispensing with the hopelessly restrictive notion of "elementary sensory experience" that is central to the traditional definition of concept-empiricism.

Hegel's point (like Kant's before him) is that we can only acquire empirical conceptions, even broadly defined, if we can identify and individuate their instances among the objects and events that surround us. The conceptions that Hegel stresses count as *pure* a priori because their possession and use is required in order to identify *any* particular object, event, or characteristic in our environs, on the sole basis of which we can learn *any* empirically based or defined conception by identifying their particular instances. Many if not most contemporary epistemologists pledge allegiance to "empiricism"; I don't expect them to welcome this category of pure a priori conceptions, although the case for them is compelling.[2]

21.2 The issue about the tenability of concept-empiricism in fact underlies the debate within logical empiricism about whether to adopt phenomenalism or physicalism as a basis for scientific discourse. Carnap initially favored phenomenalism, but already in the 1930s he and other members of the Vienna Circle were persuaded by Neurath to adopt physicalism. One main reason for this shift was to have an intersubjective

---

2. I present the case for the pure a priori status of the conception "cause" in Westphal (2003a, §3.3); for "thing" in Westphal (1998a); and for the other conceptions mentioned above in Westphal (2000a). That we have pure a priori conceptions does not, of itself, suffice to account for any knowledge we may have. However, if we have the kinds of pure a priori conceptions discussed here, it alters and alleviates many epistemological questions regarding our knowledge of commonsense objects and events. As Hume showed, the assumption that we must acquire all our conceptions from sensory experience (whether inner or outer) thwarts any prospect of understanding the everyday knowledge that we do have. (The distinction between concepts and knowledge is strictly analogous to the distinction between theory of meaning and theory of truth.) Recently, some analytic epistemologists have renewed their interest in "the a priori" (see Bealer 1999; Boghosian and Peacocke 2000), though without considering the case for pure a priori conceptions. ("Nativism" concerns inborn cognitive resources, which need not include specifically a priori conceptions or principles; one's "native" cognitive endowment could include ordinary empirical conceptions, such as "red" or "bird.")

basis for scientific communication. The general currency this shift to physicalism gained among epistemologists was canonized in Quine's (1951) declaration, in "Two Dogmas of Empiricism," that reductionism had failed. One key failure of the effort to "reduce" talk of physical objects to talk of sense data was clearly brought out by Chisholm (1957, 189–97; 1976, 138–44): in order to provide (Russellian) logical constructions of sense data to replace our talk about and knowledge of physical objects, not merely in kind but also in any and every particular instance, we must already know what physical objects there are to reconstruct, and what characteristics they have. Hence Russell's constructions presuppose the very objects and knowledge they were supposed to (re-)construct or replace.

This is a crucial problem, but there is an even more basic problem here. Identifying physical objects, even in order to substitute logical constructions for them, requires that we have the *conception,* "physical object." In "Perception," Hegel argues—soundly, I submit (see §§13.9, 22; Westphal 1998a)—that this conception cannot be defined in accord with concept-empiricism, although it is required in order to identify any particular object or event in our environs. Hence this conception is pure a priori. Consequently, with regard to this conception, like the a priori conceptions identified in "Sense Certainty," rationalists were right to contend that empiricism is an inadequate account of human knowledge. Logical constructions could replace without remainder our talk of physical objects *only if* concept-empiricism could account for our very conception of "physical object." However, the conception of "physical object" cannot be defined in accord with concept-empiricism (nor in accord with the much more liberal definition of "empirical conception" introduced in §21.1); that's the most basic reason why such replacement—why such "reductionism"—can't work.[3]

---

3. This lesson was already taught by Hume in "Of Scepticism with regard to the senses" (*Treatise* I.iv §2) (see Westphal 1989a, §4); unfortunately, twentieth-century empiricists took their lead instead from Hume's much-simplified *Enquiry Concerning Human Understanding.* Quine (1960, 116; 1961, 66, 73–4; 1969, 71; 1995, 5) recurs to that section of Hume's *Treatise,* sketching the error that Hume ascribes to us in believing that there are physical objects. This appears to be Quine's (61, 44) main reason for referring to the "myth" of physical objects. One key problem with Quine's account is that he fails to recognize that if Hume's official empiricism is true, we would lack the very concepts required to make this mistake. Quine (1969, 75; cf. 1975, 1) remains persuaded that one "cardinal tenet of empiricism remain[s] unassailable . . . to this day. . . . all inculcation of meanings of words must rest ultimately on sensory evidence." By "ultimately" Quine surely means "solely," even though sound arguments for our having some non-

22. Perceptual Synthesis and the Identification of Objects

More importantly, Hegel addressed absolutely fundamental questions regarding perceptual synthesis and our conception of the identity of perceptible things, and he pursued them much more acutely than any other philosopher (including Hume and Kant, who alone among modern philosophers recognized these issues): How is a plurality of perceptual qualities combined into the perception of some *one* object (or event)? What kind of conception of an object does such combination require? These questions arise at two levels: How are sensations coordinated to form a perceptual field within which we can identify objects? And how can we attend to and recognize the multiple features of an object so that we can identify it? These questions are fundamental to the question, What justifies such a grouping? They also concern the question, How does even a presumptive grouping occur at all, whether in mere perception or in conscious recognition of any one particular object or event? The simple coordination of sensations is a causal condition of perceptual knowledge. This causal condition is directly relevant to the normative issue of epistemic justification, because it is required to coordinate sensations *properly* in order correctly, accurately, and reliably to perceive and, ultimately, to identify objects and events in our environs. *Proper* functioning is a normative matter, because it concerns getting things right, not simply getting them processed.

Although this problem of coordinating sensations was widely overlooked in modern philosophy, it lodges centrally in the modern "new way of ideas," in "sense data" theories, and in most versions of phenomenalism. Recall that Russell's logical constructions take the "co-presence of sense data" as an undefined primitive notion. This swept the problem under the rug—or, in Wittgenstein's phrase, the conjuring trick had already been performed.[4] These questions are still current in contemporary neurophysiology of perception as the "binding problem": How do we recognize that one and the same thing (or event), rather than different things or events, stimulates various cells of a sensory organ, such as the retina?

---

logical, pure a priori conceptions, by use of which alone we can learn or acquire any empirical concepts, were developed at the turn of the nineteenth century by Kant and Hegel. Indeed, Hume himself demonstrated that his official copy theory of impressions and ideas could not at all account for the generality of thought. (I analyze this last point in some forthcoming research.)

4. Note, too, that Russell took for granted that some descriptions were definite rather than empty or ambiguous, though without posing the question, how could he know, on the basis of his own empiricist analyses of human knowledge, that those descriptions were satisfied by one and only one object?

This question arises for each sensory organ, and also regarding the relations among sensory organs. The solution to this problem constitutes a necessary condition for self-conscious experience.[5] This problem has been noted by some analytic philosophers of mind; I have found little trace of it among analytic epistemologists, despite how central it obviously is to an account of *human* perceptual knowledge.[6]

---

5. I do not claim that the "binding" of sensations is a *sufficient* condition for conscious experience; that it is a necessary condition suffices to establish its importance, and hence to establish the importance of Hegel's issue. For a comprehensive synopsis of current research on the binding problem, see Roskies (1999).

6. Price (1932, 218) papers over this issue with this observation: "In the first place, we find within this collection [*sc.* a family of all the . . . sense-data belonging to some single thing during a certain time] a certain small group which has a remarkable property. This property is that all the members of it *fit together to form a single solid* [*sc.* a complete three-dimensional figure], i.e. that taken together they form a closed three-dimensional surface, totally enclosing a certain region. Let us call the sense-data which belongs to such groups *constructible* or *spatially synthesizable* sense-data." He later notes (1932, 245) that "tactual data *supplement* the visual ones in just the way in which other visual data would supplement them if obtained by progressive adjunction." However, Price never puzzles about how we can either achieve or notice such coordination among or even within any one of our sensory modalities. Note that he (1932, 172) describes the shift from perceptual acceptance to assurance in a way that again sweeps the binding problem under the rug: "let us consider what we actually do in the case of the table. We look from various sides, from above and from underneath; we thump and grasp and stroke. That is, we replace our original sense-datum by various sorts of others . . . And if in all the new perceptual acts thus elicited a table is still presented to the mind, we become convinced that there really *is* a table." His ensuing discussion presumes rather than provides a solution to the binding problem. Price does, however, recognize that "the whole complex notion of material thinghood, in which causality is a factor" is a priori, and its use is a necessary condition for the possibility of perceptual consciousness, as distinct from mere acquaintance with sense data (1932, 102, cf. 168–9, 185–6, 306–8). Nevertheless, he does not recognize the crucial conceptual, cognitive achievement involved in ascribing (even putatively) a variety of perceived qualities to one and the same thing (or event).

Strawson (1959, 57–8, cf. 60) approaches this problem, but does not directly state or address it, when he recognizes that *de facto* correlations "between the variations of which sound is intrinsically capable and other non-auditory features of our sense-experience" are required in order to assign directions and distances to sounds on the strength of hearing alone. The existence of such correlations is crucial, but to no avail if we cannot and do not recognize them. In general, Strawson is right that recognizing them requires the conceptions of a public world and

The second question, concerning how we explicitly *recognize* various perceived characteristics as properties of any one thing, has received equally little attention from recent epistemologists, though it may be even more important and more directly relevant to epistemology because it directly concerns the kind of intellectual recognition involved in any human being's knowledge of any one perceived item. Because it is complex, I cannot pursue this issue further here. I submit, however, that Hegel's analyses of "the transcendental affinity of the manifold of intuition" (see §15) and of the conception of the identity of perceptible things (§22) suffice to show that this is both a legitimate and a tractable philosophical issue.

23. The Significance of Rejecting Reductionism

In rescinding reductionism, contemporary epistemologists conceded that concept-empiricism is false. This is a major victory for rationalism![7] However, it has not been recognized as such. In part, this is because contemporary epistemologists often disregard the traditional debates between rationalism and empiricism. (The terms are not even mentioned in Pollock [1986] or Pollock and Cruz [1999].) It is ironic, however, that Sosa (1991, 1–2) extols the liberalization of contemporary empiricism, which countenances deductive, abductive, and inductive reasoning, along

---

of reidentifiable perceptible particulars, but the link between these and actual perception involving the integration of sensations remains unaddressed.

Sellars (1968, 23–8, 230–8) comes close to the problem in discussing the role of conceptual counterpart relations to spatial or temporal relations among particulars. However, he alternates his examples of particulars between sense data or physical objects in ways that ultimately skirt the binding problem. In this, his discussion resembles Plato's *Theaetetus* (on which see Westphal 1998a, 61–2, note 211).

The construction of physical objects out of sense data does not solve this problem because it is a metaphysical puzzle that presumes rather than explains the solution to this perceptual problem (see §§21.1–22).

7. Although much of the historical debate between rationalists and empiricists focused on genetic questions of innate ideas, the semantic issue about whether all conceptions can be defined in accord with concept-empiricism was a key underlying issue; those that cannot were classified as innate. Clearly, however, Descartes focused inter alia on the semantic and epistemic issues when he argued that the wax itself cannot be known by the senses but only by the mind (Meditation 2). That rationalists were right about the inadequacy of concept-empiricism does not entail the truth of their positive epistemic views, especially those regarding innate ideas. Hegel is the grandfather of pragmatic realism, which provides an alternative to both empiricism and rationalism.

with foundations of knowledge found in rational intuitions, introspection, and direct observation of one's environment. "Empiricism" incurs such credit only against the backdrop of disregarding the demonstrable inadequacy of concept-empiricism, conjoined with an impoverished view of rationalism according to which rationalists only countenance deductive reasoning and rational intuitions as epistemic foundations (Sosa 1991, 1–2). This view of rationalism does not even accommodate Descartes, for it omits his accounts of sensation and of scientific experiment![8] Given these misunderstandings, it is little surprise that contemporary epistemologists have neglected Kant and Hegel's case for the necessity of pure a priori conceptions.

In short, it must be said, one of the key reasons why Hegel's problems are still our problems is that, although analytic epistemology has offered many insights and contributions (I am altogether sincere about these), it also has been a century-long anachronistic detour, based on disregarding the nature and developments of, inter alia, rationalist philosophy—including, most centrally, Kant's. What Strawson said some thirty years ago remains true today:

> [N]early two hundred years after they were made, [Kant's key insights] have still not been fully absorbed into the philosophical consciousness. (Strawson 1966, 29)[9]

And if most contemporary epistemologists have yet to grapple with Kant's Critical philosophy, it is no surprise that they have not grappled with Hegel's radical, pragmatic, realist transformation of it. It is a bitter irony of recent history that Hegel, who was the first to defend realism against the challenges of historicist relativism laid down by Herder, should be tarred—notoriously by Popper—as the very kind of historicist Hegel most decidedly opposed.[10]

---

8. On these topics see Clarke (1982).

9. The key insights Strawson stressed concern our ability to distinguish between the objective order of events and the subjective order of our experience of those events, and that this distinction is implicit in the conceptions under which the contents of experience are brought. In personal correspondence (1 May 1999) Strawson reaffirmed his assessment that Kant's insights still have not been adequately absorbed. In Westphal (2003c), I argue that much of the analytic work on Kant's transcendental arguments has failed to come to grips with the aim, structure, and methods of Kant's transcendental proofs.

10. On Herder's historicism, see Beiser (1987, ch. 5). On Hegel's rejection of historicism, see Beiser (1993b). On the prospect of conjoining a fallibilist, pragmatic

24. Philosophy, History, and History of Philosophy

Here a brief excursus regarding analytic philosophy, history of philosophy, and the historical character of philosophy is germane. It must be said that philosophers did not, understandably, read Russell carefully enough. Russell's exhortation to return to the eighteenth century (§21.1) was made in his reply to F. C. S. Schiller's review of *The Analysis of Mind*. In his reply, Russell indicated that his differences with Schiller were so deep that they could not be settled by logical argument without begging the question, so that "the remarks which I shall have to make will be of the nature of rhetoric rather than logic" (*CP* 9:30). In this connection Russell asserted, "I dislike the heart as an inspirer of beliefs; I much prefer the spleen" (*CP* 9:30), and excoriated romanticism, Kant, Hegel, Nietzsche, and futurism for having contributed nothing "that deserves to be remembered" (*CP* 9:41).

Russell's quick switch from logical argument to rhetorical blandishment in the face of the mere prospect of question-begging shows just how important it is to address Sextus' Dilemma of the Criterion (see Chapter 5). Unfortunately, most analytic philosophers were taken in by Russell's rhetorical invective, in part because they did not, and most could not, know that at this same time, Russell was writing very strong letters of recommendation on Schiller's behalf! (See the editorial introduction to Russell's reply, *CP* 9:37–8.) The results of Russell's invective linger in the remarkable capacity philosophers still have, as Fred Will once put it to me, no longer to understand what one says as soon as one mentions the name "Hegel."

The recent rise in Anglophone studies in the history of philosophy can be seen as a response to the unfortunate narrowing of perspective that results from historical shortsightedness. Note, for example, Hylton (1990) on Russell's early engagement with idealism, Burke (1994) on Dewey's logic, Scharff (1995) on Comte, and Ferreira (1999) on Bradley.

The most important point, however, does not concern the scope, detail, or accuracy of philosophers' express knowledge of the history of philosophy. The most important point concerns the fact—and Hegel concurs with the hermeneutical tradition in maintaining that this is a fact—that necessarily we human beings think on the basis of an often implicit, unarticulated intellectual inheritance. Contrast Wilson's point that some philosophers do, while others do not, develop their views expressly in relation to their philosophical predecessors:

---

account of justification with transcendental argument, including pure a priori conceptions, see Westphal (2003b).

In a certain sense, it is up to individual philosophers to choose our own ancestors (as Richard Rorty has said); or even to choose whether to "have" ancestors. (Wilson 1992, 209; 1999, 436)

Contrast this in turn to Kuhn's (1977, xi–xii) description of once having come, of a sudden, to think like an Aristotelian. So long as philosophers remain convinced that their thinking is sui generis, and not indebted to their intellectual inheritance, they will resist at any cost acknowledging the social dimensions of human knowledge, and also the value of Hegel's epistemology. What such philosophers overlook is that our intellectual inheritance alone enables us to think determinately and effectively, even when and as we come to modify that inheritance (see §32). Our intellectual inheritance is neither timeless conceptual bedrock, nor culturally relative blinders, nor arbitrary rules of a game; it is a corrigible set of enabling conditions for intelligent thought and action. As noted in §20, reason and tradition are neither opponents nor are they independent; they are mutually interdependent constituents of our thought and action. (McDowell [1994] acknowledges this point in connection with our "second [cultural] nature.")

Many philosophers still instinctively recoil from such ideas as these about the embeddedness of rational thought in intellectual and cultural tradition because they fear the monster of historicist relativism. Such philosophers will have difficulty distinguishing Hegel's views from historicist relativism. This is because, I venture to suggest, these philosophers are still deeply if perhaps implicitly influenced by or persuaded of the Enlightenment dichotomies criticized in §§9.1, 16, and 20. In particular, they presume that genuine rational assessment can only be based on standards that are independent of whatever is assessed—including, centrally, our intellectual and cultural inheritance. This presumption almost ineluctably leads such philosophers to espouse an essentially individualist account of justification and to disregard or even to reject out of hand the prospects of internal criticism and constructive self- and mutual criticism analyzed by Hegel and emphasized here.

Obviously, these remarks will not persuade such philosophers to think differently. I hope, however, that framing this issue explicitly may help philosophers to recognize and perhaps begin to diagnose some key issues underlying some important debates in contemporary philosophy. To the extent that these remarks are found to elucidate these debates, perhaps they may also help philosophers to recognize the ways in which contemporary philosophy once again faces some of the key dilemmas current during the Enlightenment, as discussed in §§9.1, 16, and 20. To the extent that this is recognized, these remarks may help show how, in many ways, contemporary philosophy is rooted in one central strand of our intellectual and cultural inheritance, namely, Enlightenment individualism. Recognizing any of these features of contemporary philosophy may then help show why Hegel's issues and analyses are once again of great contemporary importance.

Up to this point, I have sketched briefly a number of key points in Hegel's epistemology, along with a number of issues on which his views engage contemporary debates. Now I turn to two key features of the social dimensions of Hegel's epistemology. In Chapter 9 I argue that one prominent, resolutely individualist epistemology, Fred Dretske's information theory, cannot escape the social dimensions of human knowledge. In Chapter 10 I take up directly some basic issues in social ontology that underlie the dispute between individualists and holists. This topic raises again some of the issues just mentioned about the social dimensions of human reason and about the historical character of philosophy.

NINE

Information Theory and Social Epistemology

25. Justification through Internal Critique

In Chapter 5 I emphasized a hallmark of Hegel's account and practice of philosophical justification: positive theses can be justified only by strictly internal criticism of opposed views. This is central to his account of "determinate negation," and it introduces an important element of fallibilism into his account of justification. This is because epistemic justification is always a function of available alternatives, both historical and contemporaneous (§§10.1, 11, 28).[1] Relying solely on productive internal criticism is a very demanding requirement. However, meeting it provides very strong justification indeed. I have argued elsewhere, for example, that Hegel provides a sound internal critique of Kant's transcendental idealism, and that his account of the criteria of adequacy for theories of knowledge reveals fatal flaws both in Carnap's rejection of realism and in Putnam's cases for internal realism (Westphal 1989a, 47–67; 1996; 1998e; 2003b). These criticisms provide strong support for Hegel's realism. More specifically, these criticisms are part of his transcendental argument for mental-content externalism, which Hegel uses to support his realism (see §15).

Similarly, to justify his social account of empirical knowledge, Hegel must argue internally against nonsocial epistemologies. In this regard, his epistemology merits contemporary interest, for mainstream analytic epistemology remains highly nonsocial (i.e., individualist). One kind of epistemology designed to avoid irreducibly social factors in empirical knowledge is Dretske's information theory. Dretske's failure to avoid social factors in epistemology provides grounds that favor Hegel's social epistemology, and highlights an important feature of Hegel's social epistemology.

---

1. I reconstruct Hegel's account of such justification in Westphal (1989a, chs. 7–9); I illustrate and substantiate it by criticizing the paradigm cases of Descartes, Kant, Carnap, Alston (chs. 2–5), and Hume (Westphal 1998a). Here and in the next chapter I add at least parts of two more paradigm cases in point.

26. Key Features of Dretske's Information-Theoretic Epistemology

Dretske's (1981) title, *Knowledge and the Flow of Information* (designated "*KFI*"), indicates his concern with the transmission of information from sources of information to us as knowers via "information channels." Dretske's analysis of the conditions that channels must meet in order to serve as information channels is subtle. His main basic point is this: information channels must be reliable or "quiescent" in the sense that they are *stable;* they do not vary or change. Hence they do not themselves generate information. Information is generated by a source, because a source *does* change. Indeed, that's what a source of information *is*. If there is a stable channel between a source and a receiver, then the state of the receiver co-varies with the state of the source.[2] In this way, the receiver (ultimately, one of us) can receive information *about* the source by receiving information *from* the source via the information channel. Thus the source can be distal, even though the sensor is proximal; this is one key advance of Dretske's view over causal accounts. In Dretske's view, information is a function of eliminating alternatives. If there are only two juices in the refrigerator, and you know that one is apple and the other is orange, and you see me get the orange juice, if you pay attention, you know which kind is left in the refrigerator. According to Dretske, we only need to eliminate *relevant*, rather than all logically possible, alternatives in order to know something. On this count, Hegel agrees with Goldman (1976) and Dretske that empirical knowledge requires discrimination; to identify anything we know, we must differentiate it from other things or states of affairs. (Hegel argues for this in "Sense Certainty" and "Perception," *PhdG*, chs. 1, 2.)

Which alternative states of affairs are relevant? Between which ones must we discriminate in order to know something? Dretske's answer draws on two kinds of considerations (summarized in Dretske 1983). One is natural: What alternatives, as a matter of natural fact, are possible? What alternative states of affairs do the laws of nature allow? These facts define the range of information any source of information can generate. The other consideration is pragmatic and ultimately social: What are our needs and interests in the information? For a signal to carry information, the relevant alternatives must *be* eliminated; the signal must reliably indicate that only one of the de facto alternatives obtains. Ordinarily, to gain

---

2. It is important to note, however, that information relations are not simply causal relations of covariance (*KFI* 71–7).

knowledge by relying on a signal, we needn't be stringent about ascertaining whether those alternatives are eliminated. For example, we know that we can't distinguish Hollywood movie sets from real buildings with only a casual glance from afar. However, those sets in Hollywood pose no problem for our identifying buildings as we walk through Boston or London. However, in critical circumstances (Dretske's example is monitoring the water level in a power-generating boiler), less likely physical possibilities become relevant *to us*, and we need to take greater precautions to ensure that those possibilities are eliminated. (Recall that the relevant alternatives are *natural* possibilities, not mere logical possibilities; skeptical hypotheses don't become relevant in critical situations.)

27. Information Channels and Human Knowledge

However, Dretske treats information channels as fixed; either they exist or they don't. Although he acknowledges (Dretske 1993) that learning creates mental structures that transmit and process information, he doesn't think that this introduces a fundamentally social dimension to human thought or knowledge. Consequently, his analysis applies most directly to our sensory systems (but see §31, end). Dretske says little about the fact that human beings, as receivers and decoders of information, have information channels that are partly physiological, partly conceptual and linguistic, and partly technological (e.g., reading glasses, hearing aids, or other observational instruments or experimental apparatus). Although there is sensation and perception prior to our learning language, I submit that there is little if any perceptual *knowledge* prior to and apart from our linguistic identification of what we perceive. (Infants and animals can negotiate the world perceptually without express, propositionally formed beliefs, and hence without the propositional form of knowledge of central interest to epistemology, and especially to skepticism; cf. §13.9, end.) Explicit, linguistically based, conceptual identification is a basic part of *our* self-consciously discriminating, and thus cognitively identifying, the objects and events we perceive. "Seeing that" may have a propositional structure not found in simple "nonepistemic" seeing (Dretske 1969, part II). However, "knowing that" on the basis of "seeing that" requires giving propositional form to whatever features of our environment we may experience perceptually, and for human beings such propositional form

---

3. Dretske (*KFI* 71–7, 171–9) contends that information is inherently intensional, which he analyzes in terms of intensional opacity; this is his successor notion to the propositional structure of "seeing that." Cf. Dretske's (*KFI* 201) contrast between the absence of cognitive structure of sensory experience with

is linguistic.[3] Because they are linguistically mediated and educationally inculcated, *our* cognitive information channels are in part *social artifacts*. These social dimensions are constitutive for our cognitive information channels because their stability is established, assessed, maintained, and improved through their collective, constructive critical assessment. (Recall that stability is constitutive for an information channel, because stability is required for the channel to be quiescent, and quiescence is constitutive of information channels.)

Dretske defines knowledge in terms of beliefs caused or sustained by information. He recognizes that decoding information from a signal typically depends on a certain amount of background information we have about a source of information. He tries to avoid circularity in defining knowledge by a recursive procedure in acquiring knowledge, in which there is a basic level of first acquisition of knowledge where beliefs can be caused by information decoded without relying on background knowledge (*KFI* 86–7).[4] Two problems arise. First, although what information a signal carries may be a function of the de facto possible alternative source conditions, what information can be decoded from a signal depends on what a recipient believes or knows about the possible alternative source conditions. Second, there is no point in human *knowledge* (though surely in nascent experience) at which beliefs can be caused by information decoded without relying on background knowledge. This is because conceptions are required to form and identify one's beliefs (and their objects), and because pure a priori conceptions are required to identify and individuate any particular objects or events in our environs, which is required for us to develop empirical conceptions (sortals) of those particulars (see §§13.9, 15, 21).

Dretske's appeal to a recursive procedure masks rather than answers the key question: What is the role of language in our information processing? There must be a major role for it at a very primitive stage of human cognition. Dretske's discussion of simple conception formation

---

the cognitive structure found in digitalized information extracted from sensory experience. However, although information is inherently intensional, this intensionality does not suffice to account for the intensionality (opacity), nor the intentionality (object-directedness or "aboutness"), of our self-conscious awareness of and thought about our environs and our place and actions within it. These features of human cognizance require inferential articulation (Sellars 1981), not just opacity.

4. This is Dretske's closet positivism, as he himself once put it to our graduate student Philosophy of Science Reading Group at the University of Wisconsin-Madison, which studied *KFI* in its penultimate draft.

(e.g., "red," "robin") involves not only learning, but also both language and teaching (*KFI* 193–6). However, he doesn't pause to consider how essential are both the linguistic and the social aspects of our acquisition even of very basic conceptions. This is crucial, for Dretske argues for an externalist account of mental content, with antiskeptical results, precisely in the case of basic conceptions (*KFI* 229).[5] I submit that linguistic training is a necessary constituent in any human being's developing or acquiring representations with sufficient intensional opacity to count, in Dretske's view, as conceptions, even basic conceptions (cf. Sellars 1981). Our cognitive information channels are socially based both because they are developed into properly functioning information channels through social training, and because their reliability is maintained or (in the case of innovations) tested and established through social scrutiny (§§11, 27, 28).

Once the roles of language and social learning are acknowledged, as they must be in view of the crucial importance of both "background information" and socially learned linguistic competence in decoding signals and formulating their content expressly (propositionally), then information-theoretic epistemology faces the semantic challenges to realism proffered by coherentists and conceptual schemers. This same point holds, mutatis mutandis, for causal-reliability accounts of knowledge. This is particularly evident in causal theories that acknowledge that discrimination among distinct states of affairs is fundamental to perceptual knowledge (e.g., Goldman 1976). Of course, human beings make organic responses to the environment that differentiate among objects or events; otherwise human infants couldn't survive and natural languages would be unlearnable. As noted in §13.7, Hegel argues for this in "The Truth of Self-Certainty" (*PhdG,* part B, ch. IV). However, the vast majority of (if not all) such discriminations that count as human *knowledge,* while perceptually based, are also linguistically, and thus socially, facilitated. (This point is touched on, though admittedly all too briefly, by Plantinga [1993, 99–102].)

To respond to recent semantic challenges to realism effectively, information-theoretic epistemology needs Hegel's solution to the Dilemma of the Criterion, including his accounts of self-criticism and productive mutual criticism. I return to this point after considering Dretske's renewed attempt to evade the social dimensions of empirical knowledge.

---

5. Bieri (1989) contends that Dretske's arguments on this count are more effective than Dennett's or Davidson's. Also see Davidson (1989, 1991) regarding the social dimensions of language learning and their crucial constitutive role in coming to have propositional attitudes. These articles go at least a short way beyond issues of belief-ascription considered by Bieri.

Dretske (1993) argues that there can be nonsocially based thought in the case of animals and, by extension, humans. Dretske (1993, 192–3) also contends that learning gives rise to representations that have informational functions and that only learning can augment a creature's representational powers from simply perceiving something to believing *that* it perceives some particular kind of thing. However, Dretske's view in this essay holds only for creatures whose learning abilities are genetically determined (fixed). I submit that the learning abilities of human beings are genetically conditioned but not determined. I agree that there are cognitive representations in animals (as anyone who has seriously engaged in animal training realizes), and like Hegel (and Aristotle) I agree that human thought and cognition are based in our physiology. However, human thought and cognition also are discursive (propositionally structured) and linguistically based. Although we can learn to refine our sensory discriminations by ourselves, and thus refine the kinds of discriminations common in our culture or our specialty, the bulk of human cognitive discriminations rely on the linguistic categories we are taught as children and students. Of course insightful individuals revise old and develop new conceptions. However, such innovations are achieved *only* by using socially developed and taught skills and resources, including linguistic and conceptual resources (see §§20, 30). Moreover, one of the most important things we learn from others is *how* and *how best* to learn (cf. §11); whatever learning capacities we are genetically endowed with are developed, augmented, refined—that is, *customized*—in and by our societies (see §§28, 32). These social factors do not, however, generate the kinds of problems about explaining individual behavior that concern Dretske (1993, 187, 197), nor do they provide grounds for rejecting realism. In part, this is because natural languages are learned and developed through concurrent referential, ascriptive, and descriptive uses of terms and sentences, and such learning requires relatively stable and identifiable objects and events in our environs.[6] That there are such objects or events in

---

6. Sellars (1947; 1948; 1968, 18–9) emphasizes the role of a stable and identifiable physical environment as a requirement of learning natural languages (cf. §15). (Similar points were also made by Wittgenstein in *Philosophical Investigations*.) This simple observation shows how misguided is Richard Rorty's (1972, 17, note 1) claim that "the *whole* anti-solipsist burden is borne by the [social] 'programming,' and the 'stimuli' (like the noumenal unsynthesized intuitions) drop out" (original emphasis). This is not simply a remark in passing. Rorty (1979, 9, 170) thinks "justification" is strictly social and has nothing to do with relations between subjects and the supposed objects of their knowledge: "'Justification' [is

any world in which we can be self-conscious is the conclusion to Hegel's transcendental arguments for realism (§15) and for his externalist accounts of semantic meaning (§15) and mental content (§19).

28. Internalism and Externalism in Hegel's Epistemology

In this connection it is important to recall (§10.1) that Hegel's solution to Sextus' Dilemma of the Criterion preserves realism about the objects of knowledge without requiring us to escape our own conceptual schemes. There is no need to escape, because we're not trapped in them, even though self-conscious cognitive awareness of particulars is conceptually mediated. Hegel's solution to the Dilemma provides an analysis of the self-critical structure of consciousness. This self-critical structure of individual consciousness is augmented by exploiting the distinctions between contexts of assertion, contexts of application or action, and contexts of assessment, where these contexts are occupied by different persons or by the same person at different times. All cognitive claims can be assessed in view of their formulation, accuracy, truth, warrant, and adequacy for the purposes at hand. When others assess or adopt and use one's claims, they can generate much important corrective information, distinguishing, where need be, among the various aspects of one's consciousness of the world (see §§13.9, 27). Hegel's solution provides one important basis for the productive self-criticism and mutual criticism required to assess and revise our information channels, in their conceptual, procedural, and technical aspects. Mutual criticism is a social phenomenon and is absolutely central to our acquiring, maintaining, and improving our cognition of the world, including the very terminology we use to express our cognitive claims, evidence, and principles (§11).

A comprehensive and adequate information-theoretic epistemology must take these crucial social dimensions of knowledge into account. Dretske is right that human empirical knowledge requires reliable information channels and processing. Hegel adds that many aspects of epistemic justification derive from the socially constructed aspects of our information channels, including the whole of language, classificatory schemes, procedures of inquiry, principles—especially material principles—of infer-

---

a social phenomenon rather than a transaction between 'the knowing subject' and 'reality'"; it is "not a matter of a . . . relation between ideas (or words) and objects, but of conversation, of social practice . . . [W]e understand knowledge when we understand the social justification of belief, and thus have no need to view it as accuracy of representation." Rorty is Herder's historicist "atavar." On Rorty's self-styled pragmatism, see Haack (1998, ch. 2).

ence, and so forth. These socially based aspects of our information channels are stable and reliable, and so constitute information channels—to whatever extent they do—only because they obtain and retain their proper functioning through their ongoing collective critical scrutiny. Such scrutiny is required for determining and establishing, as best we are able, their appropriateness, adequacy, proper use, and superiority to extant alternatives. All this holds for any cognitive judgment we as individuals can and do make (see §20.4). Consequently, epistemic justification of our cognitive claims is inherently, fundamentally, and ineluctably a social phenomenon.[7]

There has been heated debate in analytic epistemology about whether epistemic justification is "externalist," "internalist," or "contextual." Epistemic justification is "externalist" if and to the extent that factors of which a cognizant subject is *un*aware play an ineliminable role in justifying a (kind of) belief or claim; for example, causal-reliability theories of perceptual knowledge. Epistemic justification is "internalist" if a cognizant subject is aware, or can readily achieve awareness, of sufficient factors that bear on the justificatory status of a belief or claim; such as foundationalist views involving perceptual appearances. Epistemic justification is "contextual" if it depends on context-specific assumptions. According to contextualists, standards of epistemic justification vary with context, rather than being uniform across all contexts. Generally, epistemologists have viewed these as competing alternatives, though some (e.g., Alston 1989, ch. 9) have advocated a mixed internalist-externalist view. Hegel

---

[7]. Brandom (1994) contends that the only way to establish the social dimensions of justification is by his radical thesis that the content of anyone's cognitive judgment is strictly a function of what *others* hold one to once one commits oneself to that judgment. This is drastic overkill, though it certainly supports his nonrealist ontology, according to which, as he put it earlier (Brandom 1979, 192), whether a kind is "objective" is *constituted* by its being treated as objective by some specified community. Brandom's (1994) semantics is an elaborate (and, to be sure, exhilarating) elaboration of Rorty's (1971, 9) suggestion that "meaningfulness depend[s] not upon a word-world connection, but upon connections between some bits of linguistic behavior and others"—as if we could behave linguistically without our embodiment or our natural environment (cf. §15). Objective kinds cannot be socially constituted, because all our social activities are rooted in the proper functioning of our neurophysiology, which can function properly only within our physical environment. To function at all, our neurophysiology must have an intrinsic natural structure that makes self-consciousness possible to begin with. Hegel's naturalism is predicated (in part) on this fact; Brandom's antinaturalism is, I believe, incompatible with it (cf. Rosenkranz 2001). No doubt Rorty would admit that brains are necessary for thinking—but only because his colleagues will let him get away with saying so, and won't let him get away without saying so.

agrees with Dretske that knowledge that p is and must be based on reliable receipt and decoding (in Hegel's view, identification by cognitive judgment) of information that p, but Hegel recognizes that externalist, internalist, and contextual factors *all* play crucial roles in epistemic justification of any and every bit of knowledge we have.[8] (Splicing Hegel's "cognitive judgment" onto Dretske's "information channel" is not forced; Dretske's distinction between analog and digital information structures [*KFI*, chs. 6, 8] maps onto Hegel's Kantian distinction between sensibility and understanding, and Dretske's account of "fully digitalized" information [*KFI* 184–5, 260] requires conceptual discrimination.)[9]

Very briefly, Hegel agrees with Dretske (and Aristotle) that the proper functioning of our neurophysiological perceptual systems—an externalist factor—is crucial to human knowledge. Likewise crucial to any of our conceptually articulated, propositionally formed cognitions are the procedures and evidence we take to be appropriate to both the formulation and to the justification of the cognitive judgment in question. Yet Hegel realizes that how we formulate and justify our cognitive judgments is conditioned (not determined) by contextual factors, including conceptual resources and available information, evidence, and techniques, both at the general level of *Weltanschauungen* and at the specific level of the kind or kinds of inquiry at issue. Hegel's account of self-criticism and mutual criticism is designed to highlight and facilitate our abilities to assess these kinds of contextual factors, at any and all levels of generality or specificity, in order to determine their appropriateness, adequacy, proper use, and superiority to known alternatives (both historical and contemporaneous) as well as we can. This is a key task of mature judgment (§11). Hegel's account of the self-critical structure of consciousness, his externalism

---

8. Some of the Hegel's recourse to reliabilism and externalism comes to the fore in his account of the significance and role of various physiological ("anthropological," he calls them) and psychological factors in human cognition (*Enz.* §§387–468; deVries 1988).

9. Kant scholars may object that Dretske allows that sensory representations are intentional, though Kant insists that intentional representations all involve concepts. This is an important point, but even granting it, it is equally important to remember that Kant insists on two distinct levels at which we use concepts: once to enable us to have intentional sensory experience at all (the synthetic work of transcendental imagination), and once again to enable us to judge what we experience cognitively (the explicit work of the understanding) (see A79/B105–6, B152, B162 note). Dretske's contrast between (analog) sensory experience and (digital) beliefs about or knowledge of what we experience parallels Kant's contrast between our sensory experience (generated in part by transcendental imagination) and our explicit cognitive judgments (understanding).

regarding mental content, and the central role he gives to mutual criticism in assessing and justifying our cognitive judgments entails that we're not trapped within our "conceptual schemes." In Hegel's view, these contextual factors and our use of them are subject to critical scrutiny and rational justification, although this is a complex social and historical process. Analytic philosophers are likely to be discomfited by mention of "*Weltanschauungen,*" because they seem too nebulous to be assessed at all. Indeed, analytic philosophy began by considering philosophical problems piecemeal in order to cut philosophical problems down to soluble size and to avoid (ultimately to scuttle) issues about *Weltanschauungen.* Unfortunately, the piecemeal approach succumbed to the semantic holism of Carnap's (1950) linguistic frameworks, and irreconcilable differences among philosophical camps were expressly instituted in the form of theoretically unjustifiable practical decisions about adopting linguistic frameworks (Wick 1951). These problems recur in the method of "reflective equilibrium" pioneered by Goodman (1965, 64) and popularized by Rawls (1971), because this method does little or nothing to guide different philosophers to the same equilibrium between principles and intuitions (even if they share substantially the same sets of each); intuitions are not sufficiently well-ordered to ground stable equilibria (Perlmutter 1998); and because there are deeply and apparently irreconcilable "intuitions" (if that is indeed what they are) among (schools of) philosophers.[10] Reflective equilibrium can scarcely avoid (sub-)cultural or historicist relativism; indeed, it may be a version of it.[11]

Early logical positivists (including Carnap, Hempel, and Ayer) were frank about their historicism. They recognized that their analyses of empirical or scientific knowledge held only for members of "our cultural circle," namely, for those who uttered relevant protocol sentences (Westphal 1989a, 56–5; cf. §18). Though the utterance of a protocol sentence had to be taken as a fact, its significance did not, because whoever uttered it could be dismissed for cause. Unfortunately, this feature of their views rapidly fell into neglect, which may partly explain why the problems with it have recently and unexpectedly resurfaced.

Hegel's theory of justification shows that we can do much more, and much better, than these methods allow. In the next and final chapter I consider a central case in point, regarding the "individualism" that has been central to the *Weltanschauung* of analytic philosophy. I shall try to show

---

10. On Rawls, see O'Neill (2003) and Reidy (1999, 2000).

11. For a more adequate account of the use of "intuitions" in improving our moral views, see Griffin (1996).

that Hegel's innovative social ontology undercuts a standard, sterile debate between individualism and holism that has supported the debate between realists and historicist relativists. Though brief, I hope to make clear how this debate has been stymied by its ideological function within two clashing twentieth-century *Weltanschauungen,* both of which are subject to critical assessment.

TEN

Methodological Individualism, Moderate Collectivism, and Social Epistemology

29. Individualism in Recent Epistemology

Mainstream epistemology has been devoutly individualist, not always in the sense given currency by Burge, that all of an individual's mental states and events can be type-identified independently of the nature of the entities in the individual's environment,[1] but in the sense that any social dimensions to human knowledge can be analyzed in accord with methodological individualism, solely in terms of the properties of and relations among individuals. However, methodological individualism in epistemology usually has been upheld on the basis of a stronger, often implicit substantive thesis, that individual knowledge of the world does not depend, in any fundamental or ineliminable way, on an individual's social relations. This assumption is found classically in Descartes and Hume, in the "ego-centric predicament" of sense data and phenomenalist views, and however implicitly, it dominates analytic epistemology with only a few quite recent and highly controversial exceptions.[2] Fortunately, Hegel provides a highly plausible social ontology, consistent with methodological individualism, that provides a much better basis for analyzing the social dimensions of human knowledge than substantive individualism, and avoids the historicist relativism that results from radical social holism (see §34).

---

1. Burge (1992, 46–7) states: "Anti-individualism is the view that not all of an individual's mental states and events can be type-identified independently of the nature of the entities in the individual's environment." Unfortunately absent from this definition are the social dimensions stressed in Burge (1979).

2. Neurath's insistence on the social character of scientific knowledge led to Carnap's and Hempel's appeal to the procedures and protocol statements of "our" cultural circle (Westphal 1989a, 56–7). One might wonder, however, whether "cultural circles" reemerge implicitly in Quine's view of one's (or "our") reassignment of truth-values across a set of statements that purportedly express the whole of a scientific account of the world (cf. Chapter 7, note 7).

30. Some Basic Problems with Individualism in Epistemology

Two basic reasons to reject the substantive individualism of traditional epistemology and to adopt a social epistemology are these. First, the traditional assumption, that everything each of us knows can be known through sources that we can assess individually, is mistaken.[3] Second, there are few if any propositions that we can know without being epistemically dependent on others.[4] This is because we depend on others to learn our language and hence to acquire the conceptions in terms of which we formulate our beliefs and cognitive claims,[5] and because we acquire our habits of forming, assessing, revising, or rejecting beliefs by training— and training is a social process (Kitcher 1994, 112).[6] It will not do to rejoin that these are merely causal antecedents of beliefs with no justificatory significance. We only have propositionally formed beliefs, we only understand the significance and implications of our beliefs, and we only know what to do with our beliefs cognitively through social training. The conceptions and skills we acquire from our communities inform in fundamental ways how we select appropriate procedures of inquiry and formulate both our evidence and our beliefs, as well as how we assess their merits; they are basic to our socially reconstructed information channels (see §§11, 20.1, 28). These are normative matters that are subject to assessment in terms of effective and adequate justification of sufficiently accurate beliefs to count, when we do well, as knowledge in the form of justified true belief.

Human cognition requires training, both linguistic training and training in identifying various objects and events in our environs, in using various methods and techniques of inquiry, and in distinguishing better from worse methods of inquiry and better from worse evidence. These forms

---

3. Kitcher (1994, 112), Coady (1992), Schmitt (1987), Kornblith (1994), Root (1998); I concur.
4. Here I concur with Kitcher (1994, 111, cf. 112), who notes that there is no "set of propositions—the individualistic basis—that we can know without reliance on others."
5. This specific point is stressed by Alston (1994), Kornblith (1994, 97, 98–9), Longino (1994), and Solomon (1994a). Kitcher (1994, 118) does not specify precisely this reason, but it is an important case in point of his more general claim about skills.
6. Kitcher speaks of "inhibiting" rather than assessing, revising, or rejecting beliefs. The causal connotations of his term are unfortunate, because they occlude the normative and judgmental dimensions of these activities (see §20.1).

of training are closely linked and are social. Consider that one basic distinction between skills and capacities is that capacities are innate characteristics that enable, for example, people to behave in various ways, whereas skills are particular kinds of behavior that are acquired, generally through training. Skills that individuals develop on their own are developed by exercising socially learned behaviors to modify their own behavior in certain regards. This parallels Alston's (1994, 30–1) point about idiosyncratic processes of belief formation: those processes are only possible because the individual has already mastered a repertoire of socially inculcated processes of belief formation. Directly or indirectly, skills result from, and so require, training, and training is a social process. To train ourselves, we must first be trained by others in various other skills, and trained in the basic procedures of training itself.

31. Some Individualist Rejoinders

The grip individualism has on our ordinary ways of thinking is reflected in the following kinds of objections.[7] For example, imagine someone who, though never having been taught to throw things, might nonetheless idly start throwing rocks at an intended target and hit the target every time. Doesn't this show that we could learn to throw by ourselves, without social aid? Well, who exactly is this supposed "we"?

The problem with this counterexample is that the someone in question isn't a human being, first because of the inhuman accuracy of this newly discovered ability; second because no human being learns to throw effectively without social training. (Witness the still-typical differences between how boys and girls throw balls—due largely to their different kinds of training.) If we want to develop an account of human knowledge (if not, why do epistemology at all?), we must devise a theory for *human*

---

7. These examples have been urged against this view by anonymous others.
8. Analytic philosophy began with firm opposition to naturalism, based on the conviction that conceptual analysis sufficed for resolving philosophical problems and was, in any event, the sole province of philosophy. This attitude held sway in epistemology until Gettier (1963) convinced epistemologists that our actual cognitive processes must be taken into account in an adequate epistemology (Kitcher 1992). Epistemologists have become a good deal more naturalistic in recent decades, but they still try to minimize their attention to actual cognitive processes. So long as they do, "Crusoe cases" will remain de rigueur (see below), developmental issues in cognition (Moore and Dunham 1995; Gopnick, Meltzoff, and Kuhl 1999) will remain neglected, and thus many of the most important social dimensions of human knowledge will remain occluded.

beings.[8] This requires acknowledging and investigating child development in its inherently social context in order to account for the social learning involved in those skills and abilities (see Chapter 9)—including those involved in inquiry and cognition—that we come, already as young adults and far too often as epistemologists, to take for granted. I do not deny that an individual can develop a new skill on his or her own; my point is that he or she can do so only by using other socially acquired skills and abilities. Even if the proposed counterexample were made more realistic by supposing someone developing an accurate throw solo by trial and error, I submit that human beings who have the ability to refine any skill solo have that ability only on the basis of social training to conceive a plan of training, to persist in its execution, and to profit from critical assessment of their performance.

Other individualist objections are reflected in this kind of question: What is the social dimension of the skill of opening a window? The answer is that different societies produce different kinds of window mechanisms that require somewhat different knowledge and skill to operate. (I'm reminded of this frequently when visiting unfamiliar buildings abroad, especially recent construction in Germany.) To the extent that the act of opening the window is intentional, the aim of and appropriate conditions for opening a window are socially mediated also by education and etiquette.

"Crusoe cases" are no better than Putnam's (c. 1978) supercomputers that fell from the sky. Disregarding genetic origins results in views that do not accurately or adequately reflect the nature and capacities—and limits—of the phenomena in question, including human cognizers. Robinson Crusoe was raised and educated in England before setting sail and long before being shipwrecked. Without that social training, he would not have had the skills to assess his circumstances nor the abilities to plan and to act to preserve himself. Consider that there is even a social element in the development of our perceptual abilities: cultures using curved rather than rectilinear structures either don't experience the Müller-Lyer illusion, or do so with little distortion (Hundert 1989, 269–70). Concerns and objections like these show that substantive individualism is rooted much more deeply in philosophic thought than is justified; so much so that epistemologists really ought to reflect on the social and historical inculcation of the fervent belief in this kind of individualism.[9]

---

9. Notice, for example, that substantive individualism remains central to Goldman's work. He views epistemology as divided into two nearly distinct subfields: individual (Goldman 1986) and social (Goldman 1999) epistemology. The only individual mental operations that belong to Goldman's (1999, ch. 4) social epistemology are the ways one reasons on the basis of others' testimony. Notice, too,

32. Individualism, Holism, and Hegel's Moderate Collectivism

As mentioned, the traditional and prevailing reason for resisting social analyses of knowledge is the fear, represented in Hegel's day by Herder's historicist relativism, that a social account of knowledge must reject realism.[10] This fear is supported by the widespread, though often implicit, assumption that there is only one contrast between "individualism" and "collectivism" (setting aside as irrelevant here Burge's use of the term "individualism" for strictly internalist accounts of mental content). Hegel's social ontology undermines this specious dichotomy.

Hegel's social ontology, which I call "moderate collectivism," can be summarized in three theses:

MC1. Individuals are fundamentally social practitioners. Everything a person does, says, or thinks is formed in the context of social practices that provide material and conceptual resources, objects of desire, skills, procedures, techniques, and occasions and permissions for action, et cetera.

MC2. What individuals do depends on their own response to their social and natural environment.

MC3. There are no individuals, no social practitioners, without social practices, and, vice versa, there are no social practices without social practitioners, without individuals who learn, participate in, perpetuate, *and who modify* those social practices as needed to meet their changing needs, aims, and circumstances (including procedures and information).

This is the kind of view we should expect of Hegel: where others see only an exclusive dichotomy, Hegel identifies a biconditional relation.[11]

---

that individualist assumptions undergird Kripke's (1982) interpretation of Wittgenstein's view of rule-following as a "skeptical solution." The social dimensions of Wittgenstein's view of rule-following (Savigny 1991; Will 1997, chs. 7–9) are opaque to Kripke.

10. Today these fears are often associated with the Strong Programme in the sociology of knowledge. However, this Programme has evolved significantly (Barnes, Bloor, and Henry 1996) and is more sophisticated than is often recognized. For a conspectus of contemporary science studies, see Biagioli (1999). For a good discussion of constructivism in the history of science, see Golinski (1998).

11. See Westphal (1989a, 169–70, 176; 1994). Hegel's moderate collectivism is also fundamental to his social theory (Westphal 1993, esp. 235–7). For a general discussion of this view (though not under this name), see DeGeorge (1983).

Let me try to clarify and, at least to some extent, recommend Hegel's view, which is prone to various misunderstandings. One misunderstanding is to assume that our social context determines or is sufficient to explain the thought and behavior of an individual. This is radical holism, not MC1. Moderate collectivism emphasizes how our social context conditions but does not determine what we say or think, in part because our social context provides us with rich resources that enable us to think or behave at all in specific and often creative ways. To fear social conditions as, or as entailing, *constraints* is a fundamental error. Social conditions can provide constraints, even unfortunate ones. (Crime prevention is a fortunate social constraint, is it not?) However, many of the most important and fundamental social conditions are *enabling* conditions; they are guides, not chains. Simply noting this fact is unlikely to persuade, but it may point to one important change in perspective that is required to appreciate the social bases of human thought and action.

The fear of social conditions as determinants generates puzzlement about MC2: How can individuals fashion "their own" responses to their social or natural environment, if their thoughts and actions depend so deeply on their environment? Individual inventiveness stems in part from fortunate mis-interpretation or mis-understanding, and in part from creative reconfiguration of available social or natural resources. There is no creation ex nihilo among human beings, but this hardly entails that there is no human creativity! Human creativity lies in transformation, often strikingly novel transformation, of available resources.

It may help to recall that Einstein's revolution began with a rather humble shift in viewpoint. He began with the fact that Lorentz provided two structurally quite distinct formulae for calculating the current generated in a coil of wire. One formula concerned a magnet that moved with respect to the coil in which the current was generated; the other formula concerned a coil that moved with respect to a magnet. This anomaly was recognized at the time; students of electrodynamics were made aware of it by their teachers. It occurred to Einstein to take the asymmetries between the two Lorentz equations not as a mere oddity but as a serious anomaly to be resolved. The resources Einstein used were socially developed and transmitted to him, and he drew upon those social resources—including constructive mutual criticism—throughout his radical transformation of them into one of the most important and revolutionary theoretical developments of all time.[12]

---

12. Cf. Will's (1997, 102) parallel example of Lisa Meitner's contribution to nuclear physics.

Moderate collectivism is a (broadly, not reductively) naturalistic view; it is consistent with the fact that people have natural, innate (genetic, physiological, and psychological) traits,[13] and it stresses the central importance of our actual processes and activities for understanding the nature, scope, and limits of justification, whether in cognition or action (Kitcher 1992). It points out that whatever natural needs, ends, and capacities people have are *literally* customized by the social and natural environments in which they develop. Individuals satisfy their needs, form their specific desires, and act to achieve their particular ends (whether practical or theoretical) by acting toward objects made available to them by their societies and by acting in ways (using skills and procedures) made available to them by their societies. This is a different *kind* of individualism; a different way of conceiving human individuals. Its mere possibility shows that there is no *single* contrast within social ontology between "individualism" and "holism." Once the basic reasons for adopting a social epistemology are recognized (§§27, 28, 30), moderate collectivism should recommend itself, not merely as possible but as altogether plausible.

Positive proof of moderate collectivism requires showing, on a case-by-case basis, that everything one does, says, or thinks is formed in the context of social practices that provide material and conceptual resources, objects of desire, skills, procedures, and the like. No one acts on the general, merely biological needs for food, safety, companionship, or sex; no one seeks food, safety, companionship, or sex in general. Rather, one acts on much more specific needs for much more specific kinds of objects that fulfill those needs, and one acts to achieve one's aims in quite specific ways. One's society deeply conditions (though does not determine) one's ends and abilities—and, of course, how one conceives them—because it provides specific objects that meet, or materials for meeting, those ends, and it specifies and provides procedures for obtaining or employing them. Similarly, how one thinks is conditioned (though not determined) by the conceptions, beliefs, procedures of inquiry, and principles of reasoning one learns from one's society (Alston 1994; Kornblith 1994; Kitcher 1994).

33. Substantive Individualism in Recent Epistemology

The longstanding attempt to analyze human knowledge in strictly individualist terms is committed not simply to methodological individualism

---

13. Including, e.g., the language instinct brilliantly defended by Pinker (1994). It is instinctive for humans to learn a language; which language they learn is socially conditioned. Regarding 'broad' naturalism, see Rouse (2002).

but to substantive individualism, namely, the view that the (basic) cognitive states or abilities of individuals can be understood fully and adequately without recourse to interpersonal or social phenomena. Social relations are, in this view, cognitively inessential. This attempt has failed (§§27, 28, 30, 32). Methodological individualism holds that all social phenomena must be understood in terms of the behavior and dispositions of individuals—*and their relations*.[14] Strictly speaking, this thesis only denies transhuman social agents. Debate about it has been protracted and inconclusive in part because many theorists have upheld under its banner either or both of two stronger substantive theses: that individuals have "primacy" over social relations, or that all social phenomena can be defined, explained in terms of, or "reduced to" the nonsocial characteristics of individuals.[15] These are two versions of substantive, "atomistic" individualism. Strictly speaking, *methodological* individualism does not entail atomistic individualism, nor does it entail the "primacy" of individuals over societies. Methodological individualism is consistent with moderate collectivism. Though substantive individualism has failed in epistemology (§§27, 28, 30, 32), the most important grounds for recognizing the social dimensions of human knowledge accord with and support moderate collectivism, not radical holism. Contrary to widespread supposition, recognizing that social relations are (in the present case, cognitively) essential to human individuals does not entail a radical holism that grants communities primacy over their members, nor does it require rescinding either methodological individualism or realism in epistemology.

34. Holism and Hegel's Moderate Collectivism

Hegel's own views have been seriously misunderstood by uncritical holists (and their often hypocritical critics), who have contributed much more heat than light to this debate. Indeed, Hegel has been discredited by many of his would-be advocates. Phillips' (1976) analysis of holism is very use-

---

14. Kitcher (1994, 116) speaks of analyzing collective phenomena in terms of "the properties and relations among" individuals; his point is the same although the phrasing is slightly different.

15. See Mandelbaum (1973), Goldstein (1973), Brodbeck (1973). Note Kitcher's (1994, 116) reference, in connection with methodological individualism, to the issue of whether social phenomena are irreducibly collective. One key point of moderate collectivism is that social phenomena can be "irreducibly" collective— i.e., inherently social, *inter*-personal—without being radically holistic.

ful here. Of the key theses he identifies, Hegel is committed only to some of the five theses comprised in Phillips' "Holism I":

> I.1 The analytic approach as typified by the physico-chemical sciences proves inadequate when applied to certain cases—for example, to a biological organism, to society, or even to reality as a whole.
>
> I.2 The whole is more than the sum of its parts.
>
> I.3 The whole determines the nature of its parts.
>
> I.4 The parts cannot be understood if considered in isolation from the whole.
>
> I.5 The parts are dynamically interrelated or interdependent. (Phillips 1976, 6)

Of these theses, Hegel is committed to I.2 (the whole is more than the sum of its parts), *provided* that this is understood to comment on "sum" rather than on any alleged transcendence of the whole with respect to its parts; to I.4 (the parts cannot be adequately understood if considered in isolation from the whole); and to I.5 (the parts are dynamically interrelated or interdependent). Hegel is committed also to a modified version of I.3, namely:

> I.3′ The whole conditions [not "determines"] the nature of its parts.

By MC3, however, Hegel also holds that the whole is conditioned by the nature of its parts. Hence Hegel rejects radical holism and accepts an analytical approach to studying holistic phenomena (*pace* I.1; cf. *Rph* §189R, where Hegel extols the insights of the Scottish political economists, which provide one crucial basis for his political philosophy). Hegel opposes reductionism, but he insists that a holistic phenomenon must be understood in terms of its parts or aspects—in their interrelations. To this extent Hegel only accepts part of Phillips' "Holism II":

> II. A whole, even after it is studied, cannot be explained in terms of its parts; opposed by reductionism. (Phillips 1976, 36)

Hegel rejects reductionism, but (as already noted) he thinks that wholes and their parts are mutually interdependent, so that a "whole" must be explained in terms of its parts—in their interrelations. Hegel merely denies that genuine wholes can be understood exclusively in terms of their dissociated parts.

Hegel does espouse Phillips' "Holism III":

> III. It is necessary to have terms referring to wholes and their properties. (Phillips 1976, 37)

Phillips notes that this thesis can be accepted by devotees of the analytic method and of reductionism. He (1976, 122–3) further notes that all of this is eminently reasonable. Note, however, that there is room for several options regarding "the" analytical method (viz., whether it is held to require reductionism) and regarding the reasons supporting Holism III.[16] Fortunately, this brief review should provide sufficient basis to indicate (in the next two sections) some of the merits of Hegel's moderate collectivism.

35. Moderate Collectivism and "the" Subject of Knowledge

If moderate collectivism is true, then the "community" does not form a supraindividual subject of knowledge. Individuals are subjects of knowledge in the sense that individual people have, develop, assess, modify, and reject beliefs. The fact that the content and justification of any individual's beliefs depend (directly and indirectly) on socially accrued evidence and socially learned conceptions, intellectual norms, and critical practices (all of which are among our most important information channels) commits us only to moderate collectivism, not to radical holism.[17] This point is further supported by the third main reason to adopt a social account of knowledge, namely, that justification is ultimately (though not solely!) a fallible and corrigible product of mutual critical scrutiny.[18] Individuals have beliefs; but what beliefs they have and what justification those beliefs have—indeed the very fact that individuals have propositionally formed beliefs that are subject to questions and answers about their content and justification—is a function both of that individual's inquiry *and* the cognitive resources supplied to that individual by his or her community (see §§11, 24, 27). Insisting that either the individual or the community is "primary" greatly obscures the central issues, especially in view of how little attention has been given to what this "primacy" is supposed to consist in. Although radical holism leads inevitably to histori-

---

16. Fortunately, methodology in the social sciences has developed beyond the earlier, often ill-formed debates; see, for example, Bohman (1991).

17. This is fundamental to Longino's (1994) social analysis of knowledge. She summarizes very nicely the basic requirements for forming legitimate, and *legitimating*, consensus through mutual critical evaluation, as well as the social dimensions of "observation" in scientific contexts.

18. Unfortunately, this important thesis cannot be developed further here. See §§11, 20, 24, 27, 38, 30, and the previous note.

cist relativism, moderate collectivism is consistent with epistemological realism.[19]

36. Hegel's Moderate Collectivism versus "Plural Subjects"

Both the point and the plausibility of Hegel's moderate collectivist epistemology can be highlighted by contrasting it with Schmitt's (1994b) analysis of group knowledge. Schmitt identifies some cases of knowledge possessed by a group where the individuals in that group have that knowledge only as members of that group. His social analysis of justified true group beliefs is based on Gilbert's analysis of collective belief, an analysis that also attempts to identify an intermediate position between atomistic individualism and radical holism. Her analysis is based on defining a plural subject as follows:

> For persons A and B and psychological attribute X, A and B form a *plural subject* of X-ing if and only if A and B are jointly committed to X-ing as a body, or, if you like, as a single person. (Gilbert 1994, 244)

As Schmitt (1994b, 259–60) notes, Gilbert directly qualifies this basic thought in three crucial ways: first, the definition just quoted differs from atomistic individualism by recognizing that groups (of this sort) only exist insofar as some number of people are expressly committed *jointly* to intending to do something. Second, individual intentions to act solo, no matter how well coordinated or faithfully executed, do not suffice. However, third, this view also differs from radical holism by denying that the group has any "mind" above or in addition to the minds of its members.

Moderate collectivism is superior to Gilbert's plural subjects as a basis for social epistemology. Her plural subjects require relatively mature individuals because members of her plural subjects must be intellectually sophisticated enough to form a joint intention, which requires (on her analysis) recognizing one's own and one's fellow group members' joint intentions to do something jointly. Her analysis thus makes group membership entirely and explicitly voluntary. However, the social dimensions

---

19. Hegel's views are, to this extent at least, consistent with Kitcher's. Unfortunately, Kitcher's (1994) analysis is insufficiently clear about the distinction between methodological and substantive individualism; he does not specify what sort of "primacy" is supposedly at issue in the debates between individualists and collectivists (1994, 113), and hence he does not recognize Hegel's via media, moderate collectivism.

of human knowledge set in much earlier than this level of relative intellectual maturity (see §§11, 27, 28, 30). The social dimensions of knowledge set in as we learn conceptions in our linguistic communities and as we learn from our cognitive communities to form, assess, hold, revise, or relinquish beliefs. (At the early stages, these are the same communities in two related capacities.) Gilbert's analysis is useful, but not epistemically fundamental.

Schmitt (1994b, 272–6) does identify a genuine case of collective knowledge on the part of plural subjects: courts of law. However, because Schmitt's analysis focuses only on voluntarily formed plural subjects, it cannot analyze the most fundamental social dimensions of human knowledge. His analysis addresses an important subtopic in social epistemology that might best be called "corporate epistemology." Moderate collectivism emphasizes the fact that human cognition is based in conceptual and investigative skills and information that are provided to us by our social groups from the beginning as we grow up, acquire language and information, learn, study, and inquire.

37. The Barrenness of the "Individualism–Holism" Dispute

The longstanding supposition that "individualism" and "holism" form a single, exclusive, and exhaustive contrast is conceptually unfounded. I submit that an honest appraisal of the relevant data also shows that it is factually unfounded. However durable and ideologically "useful" this contrast has been, it is long overdue for discard on the scrap heap of history. Once epistemologists and other social theorists liberate themselves from the restrictive and misleading issue of the "primacy" of individuals or communities, they can recognize the importance of moderate collectivism for developing a socially and historically grounded epistemological realism. This idea has a rich philosophical history running from Hegel through American Pragmatism to the present day.[20] Unfortunately, this

---

20. A socially grounded realism is central to Peirce's first distinctively pragmatic writings. It results jointly from what Peirce (1877, 1878; cf. 1905) calls "the hypothesis of science" and the communal character of scientific inquiry, including the communal nature of scientific evaluation of scientific results. Dewey's (1930) commitment to moderate collectivism is explicit. This view is fundamental for his account of knowledge (i.e., "inquiry"). The social role of mutual criticism in epistemic justification is implied by his account of philosophical problems and his instrumentalist theory of value (Dewey 1939, 1948). The most important and explicit writings in this pragmatist tradition of socially grounded realism are Will

idea has been occluded by a pervasive though faulty dichotomy between "individualism" and "holism."[21] The untenability of this dichotomy was obscured, in part, by the anxieties and exigencies of the cold war.[22] Now that this ideological battle is subsiding (despite vigorous efforts in some quarters recently to revive it), perhaps philosophers may finally come to appreciate Hegel's acute epistemology, which is even more important today than when he developed it. The social dimensions of empirical knowledge has become a hot topic in history and philosophy of science and even in more mainstream epistemology (e.g., Goldman 1999). I do not wish to suggest that Hegel anticipated all the fascinating results of these inquiries. I do contend that Hegel provides an especially important framework for understanding, inter alia, the nature and importance of the social dimensions of human knowledge (see Chapters 6 and 7, and §§11, 27, 28, 30). I hope that this synopsis has helped to make Hegel's method, framework, and epistemological views more intelligible and compelling.

(1974, 1988, 1997). For good discussions of recent work in pragmatic realism, see Hare (1998), Shook (2003).

21. Developing a moderate collectivist epistemology requires reinvestigating issues formerly debated under the heading of "internal" and "external" relations, but this need not be regretted; that debate too was stymied by unnecessarily extreme positions (see Horstmann 1984). Horstmann's excellent study deserves much more attention than it has received.

22. It is not too much to say that the major hot and cold wars of the preceding century were fought between powers committed to radical holism (fascists of the far right and left) and centrists committed to liberal individualism. That context understandably made it difficult to distinguish perspicuously between radical holism and moderate collectivism. This lack of perspicacity is part of what regrettably extruded the moderate collectivist liberalism of T. H. Green from the twentieth-century tradition of Anglophone philosophy.

Recommended Readings

The following guide aims to link Hegel's *Phenomenology* to useful secondary literature in English, in accord with the interpretation sketched in this book. Hence this guide is quite selective and focused. I welcome suggestions from readers regarding other pertinent materials.[1]

Books

1. Introductions to Hegel's Philosophy

J. Royce, *Lectures on Modern Idealism* (New Haven: Yale University Press, 1919), Lectures VI–IX. Concisely sets Hegel's context.

Stephen Houlgate, *Freedom, Truth and History: An Introduction to Hegel's Philosophy* (London: Routledge, 1991). Houlgate's book is a moderately sized introduction to Hegel for nonspecialists. His presentation is clear, accessible, and judicious. Houlgate's aim requires a style that is more expository than analytical, more comparative than argumentative; his interpretation is generally balanced and accurate. (A new, revised edition is forthcoming from Blackwell.)

Justus Hartnack, *From Radical Empiricism to Absolute Idealism* (Lewiston/Queenston: Mellen, 1986). Hartnack places Hegel's *Phenomenology* in the context of Hume, Kant, and his immediate predecessors, Fichte and Schelling. A very useful philosophical introduction for anyone with some background in modern philosophy.

Justus Hartnack, *An Introduction to Hegel's Logic,* K. R. Westphal, ed., L. Aagaard-Mogensen, tr. (Indianapolis: Hackett, 1998). The title indicates that this book focuses on Hegel's *Logic,* though many of Hartnack's topics bear on major themes and issues throughout Hegel's philosophy, including the *Phenomenology.* Both of Hartnack's books are clear, concise, and generally accurate—rare qualities among the vast literature on Hegel's philosophy.

Frederick Beiser, *Hegel,* Routledge Philosophers series (Routledge: forthcoming, c. 2004). A substantial study covering a wide range of

---

1. Readers seeking a broader range of material on Hegel's *Phenomenology* will find good selections of it collected in Stern (1993) and Lamb (1998). A comprehensive bibliography of Hegel literature up to 1975 is found in Steinhauer and Hausen (1980). A vast selected bibliography on Hegel's *Phenomenology* is found in Harris (1997), 2:784–868.

topics and texts in Hegel's philosophy, especially those pertaining to issues discussed in the present study; supplants all prior such works.

2. Comprehensive Commentaries

Henry Harris, *Hegel's Ladder*, 2 vols. (Indianapolis: Hackett, 1997). This is the only truly comprehensive commentary on Hegel's *Phenomenology*. It is authoritative and should be consulted on any and all topics in the *Phenomenology*, aside from epistemology. On some shortcomings of Harris' commentary, see

K. R. Westphal, "Harris, Hegel, and the Spirit of the *Phenomenology*," *Clio* 27.4 (1998):551–72.

K. R. Westphal, "Hegel, Harris, and Sextus Empiricus," *Owl of Minerva* 31.2 (2000):155–72.

K. R. Westphal, *Hegel's Epistemological Realism* (Dordrecht: Kluwer, 1989). Complementing Harris' commentary, this is the only comprehensive and detailed analysis of Hegel's epistemology in the *Phenomenology*. (Referred to subsequently as "*HER*.")

3. Introductions to Hegel's *Phenomenology*

Robert Stern, *Hegel and the Phenomenology of Spirit* (London: Routledge, 2001). A very useful student's guide to the *Phenomenology*.

Quentin Lauer, *A Reading of Hegel's Phenomenology of Spirit* (New York: Fordham, 1976). Lauer's analysis falters at various places, but his book has the enormous advantage over other introductions that it provides a genuine *reading* of Hegel's *text*. Thus it avoids the fate of other synopses, namely, that instead of explicating Hegel, the author substitutes his own ideas about what Hegel supposedly did or ought to have said.

M. Forster, *Hegel's Idea of a Phenomenology of Spirit* (Chicago: University of Chicago Press, 1998). A detailed attempt to explain Hegel's phenomenological project. Marred by some epistemological omissions, but otherwise very useful. For a précis, see the review by Merold Westphal, *Philosophy and Phenomenological Research* 65.2 (2002):476–8.

Specific Further Recommended Readings

4. Hegel's Context

W. Kaufmann, "Chronology" of Hegel's Period, in *Hegel: A Reinterpretation* (New York: Doubleday, 1966), xxi–v.

F. C. Beiser, "Hegel's Historicism," in F. C. Beiser, ed., *A Companion to Hegel* (Cambridge: Cambridge University Press, 1993), 270–300.

5. Problems with Translation

   H. Kainz, "Some Problems with the English Translations of Hegel's 'Phänomenologie des Geistes'," *Hegel-Studien* 21 (1986):175–82.

6. Hegel's Problematic

   K. R. Westphal, "Problems of Knowledge and Problems with Epistemology," *HER*, ch. 1.

7. Hegel's Introduction to the *Phenomenology*

   Translation: K. R. Westphal, *HER*, Appendix I.

   Analysis: K. R. Westphal, "Hegel's Solution to the Dilemma of the Criterion," in J. Stewart, ed., *The Phenomenology of Spirit Reader: A Collection of Critical and Interpretive Essays* (Albany: State University of New York Press, 1998), 76–91.

8. Charts of the Structure of Hegel's *Phenomenology*

   Above, §14.

   K. R. Westphal, "The Triadic Structure of the *Phenomenology of Spirit*," *HER*, Appendix III, 201–3.

   A. Kojève, Appendix, *Introduction to the Reading of Hegel* (New York: Basic Books, 1969), 263–87.

9. Analysis of the Structure of Hegel's *Phenomenology*

   K. R. Westphal, "The Structure of Hegel's Argument in the *Phenomenology of Spirit*," *HER*, ch. 11, 149–88.

   Jon Stewart, "The Architectonic of Hegel's *Phenomenology of Spirit*," in *idem.*, ed., *The Phenomenology of Spirit Reader* (op. cit.), 444–77.

10. The "Consciousness" Section: "Sense-Certainty"; "Perception"; "Force and Understanding"

    C. Taylor, "The Opening Arguments of the *Phenomenology*," in A. MacIntyre, ed., *Hegel: A Collection of Critical Essays* (Notre Dame: University of Notre Dame Press, 1976), 151–88.

K. R. Westphal, "Hegel's Internal Critique of Naïve Realism," *Journal of Philosophical Research* 25 (2000):173–229.

K. R. Westphal, "'Sense Certainty,' or Why Russell Had No 'Knowledge by Acquaintance,'" *Bulletin of the Hegel Society of Great Britain* 47/48 (2004):110–23.

K. R. Westphal, "Hegel's Attitude toward Jacobi in the 'Third Attitude of Thought toward Objectivity'," *Southern Journal of Philosophy* 27.1 (1989):135–56.

K. R. Westphal, "Hegel and Hume on Perception and Concept-Empiricism," *Journal of the History of Philosophy* 33.1 (1998): 99–123. A précis of the following item.

K. R. Westphal, *Hegel, Hume und die Identität wahrnehmbarer Dinge; Historisch-kritische Analyse zum Kapitel "Wahrnehmung" in der Phänomenologie von 1807* (Frankfurt am Main: Klostermann, 1998). "Hegel, Hume, and the Identity of Perceptible Things." A comprehensive reconstruction and evaluation of Hegel's chapter, "Perception" (*PhdG*, ch. 2), showing that Hegel develops a sophisticated internal critique of Hume's concept-empiricism in "Of Scepticism with regard to the senses" (*Treatise of Human Nature*, I.iv §2).

K. R. Westphal, "Hegel, Philosophy, and Mathematical Physics," *Bulletin of the Hegel Society of Great Britain* 36 (1997):1–15.

W. deVries, "Hegel on Reference and Knowledge," *Journal of the History of Philosophy* 26.2 (1988):297–307.

W. deVries, "Hegel on Representation and Thought," *Idealistic Studies* 17.2 (1987):123–32. DeVries' essay touches on the epistemological significance of Hegel's ontology, adumbrated in "Force and Understanding," and on the social dimensions of Hegel's view of thought, which is developed in the remainder of the *Phenomenology;* see deVries' remarks about "demands and permissions."

11. Hegel's Ontology and Philosophy of Nature (in connection with "Force and Understanding" and "Observing Reason")

T. Wartenberg, "Hegel's Idealism," in F. C. Beiser, ed., *A Companion to Hegel* (op. cit.), 102–29.

K. R. Westphal, "Hegel's Idealism and Epistemological Realism," *HER,* ch. 10, 140–8.

K. R. Westphal, "On Hegel's Early Critique of Kant's *Metaphysical Foundations of Natural Science,*" in S. Houlgate, ed., *Hegel and* the *Philosophy of Nature* (Albany: State University of New York Press, 1998), 137–66.

K. R. Westphal, "Hegel, Philosophy, and Mathematical Physics," *Bulletin of the Hegel Society of Great Britain* 36 (1997):1–15.

G. Buchdahl, "Hegel's Philosophy of Nature," *British Journal for the Philosophy of Science* 23 (1972):257–90.

G. Buchdahl, "Hegel's Philosophy of Nature and the Structure of Science," in M. Inwood, ed., *Hegel* (London: Oxford University Press, 1985), 110–36.

G. Buchdahl, "Conceptual Analysis and Scientific Theory in Hegel's Philosophy of Nature (with special reference to Hegel's optics)," in R. Cohen and M. Wartofsky, eds., *Hegel and the Sciences,* Boston Studies in the Philosophy of Science (Dordrecht: Reidel, 1984), 13–36.

B. Beaumont, "Hegel and the Seven Planets," *Mind* 62 (1954):246–8.

12. On "Self-Consciousness"

F. Neuhouser, "Deducing Desire and Recognition in the *Phenomenology of Spirit,*" *Journal of the History of Philosophy* 24 (1986): 243–62.

F. Neuhouser, "Fichte and the Relation between Right and Morality," in D. Breazeale and T. Rockmore, eds., *Fichte: Historical Context/ Contemporary Controversies* (New York: Humanities Press, 1994), 158–80.

F. Beiser, "Solipsism and Intersubjectivity," *Hegel* (Routledge: forthcoming), ch. 6.

J. Shklar, "Independence and Dependence," *Freedom and Independence: A Study of Hegel's Phenomenology of Mind* (Cambridge: Cambridge University Press, 1976), ch. 2, 57–73 (only).

M. Forster, "Skeptical Culture," in *idem., Hegel and Skepticism* (Cambridge, Mass.: Harvard University Press, 1989), part II.

13. On "Reason"

13.1 On Hegel's critique of Kant, Fichte, and Schelling in the introduction to "Reason":

K. R. Westphal, "Kant, Hegel, and the Transcendental Material Conditions of Possible Experience," *Bulletin of the Hegel Society of Great Britain* 33 (1996):23–41.

K. R. Westphal, "Kant, Hegel, and the Fate of 'the' Intuitive Intellect," in S. Sedgwick, ed., *The Reception of Kant's Critical Philosophy: Fichte, Schelling, and Hegel* (New York: Cambridge University Press, 2000), 283–305.

13.2 On §VA "Observing Reason" (also see §11):

A. MacIntyre, "Hegel on Faces and Skulls," in *idem.*, ed., *Hegel* (op. cit.), 219–36.

H. B. Acton, "Hegel's Conception of the Study of Human Nature," in Inwood, ed., *Hegel* (op. cit.), 137–52, §I.

13.3 On §§VB and C:

J. Shklar (op. cit.), "The Moral Failures of Asocial Men," ch. 3.

13.4 On §VC:

D. Hoy, "Hegel's Critique of Kantian Morality," *History of Philosophy Quarterly* 6.2 (1989):207–32.

14. On "Spirit"

14.1 On §§VIA and B:

J. Shklar (op. cit.), "The Life Cycle of a Culture," 74–95 and ch. 4.

M. Forster, *Hegel and Skepticism* (op. cit.), "Skeptical Culture in Hegel's Philosophy of History," 47–94.

14.2 On "Pure Insight":

A. M. Wilson, "Encyclopédie," *Encyclopedia of Philosophy*, P. Edwards, ed. in chief (New York: Collier MacMillan, 1967), 2:505–8.

14.3 On §VIC "Self-Certain Spirit; Morality":

K. R. Westphal, "Hegel's Critique of Kant's Moral World View," *Philosophical Topics* 19.2 (1991):133–76.

M. Gram, "Moral and Literary Ideals in Hegel's Critique of 'The Moral World-View'," *Clio* 7.3 (1978):375–402; rpt. in J. Stewart, ed., *The Phenomenology of Spirit Reader* (op. cit.), 307–33.

J. Shklar (op. cit.), "Beyond Morality: A Last Brief Act," ch. 5.

14.4 On Hegel's Social Ontology:

R. DeGeorge, "Social Reality and Social Relations," *Review of Metaphysics* 37 (1983):3–20. DeGeorge sets out Hegel's view, though he does not mention Hegel.

K. R. Westphal, tr. and ed., "Community as the Basis of Free Individual Action," Translation and annotation of excerpts from

Hegel's *Phenomenology of Spirit*, in M. Daly, ed., *Communitarianism* (Belmont, Calif.: Wadsworth, 1994), 36–40.

15. On Hegel's Social Account of Assertion and Assessment

    Hegel presents this topic in "Conscience" in terms of moral judgment, but it is general enough to apply to cognition as well.

    R. Brandom, "Freedom and Constraint by Norms," *American Philosophical Quarterly* 16,3 (1979): 187–96. One caveat: Brandom's views on the social constitution of "objective kinds" are not Hegel's.

16. On "Religion"

    Q. Lauer, "Religion," *A Reading of Hegel's Phenomenology of Spirit* (op. cit.), ch. 8, §A ff., 234–55 (only).

    G. di Giovanni, "Faith without Religion, Religion without Faith: Kant and Hegel on Religion," *Journal of the History of Philosophy* 41 (2003):

17. On "Absolute Knowing"

    K. R. Westphal, "The Structure of Hegel's Argument in the *Phenomenology*," *HER*, ch. 11.

18. On the "Preface"[2]

    W. Kaufmann, Preface, translation with generous annotations in *Hegel: Texts and Commentary* (New York: Doubleday, 1966).

    R. Schacht, "A Commentary on the Preface to Hegel's *Phenomenology of Spirit*," in *Hegel and After* (Pittsburgh: University of Pittsburgh Press, 1975), ch. 3.

---

2. I mention the Preface here because Hegel wrote it after completing the *Phenomenology,* and in anticipation of completing his "system of philosophical science" (as he then conceived it) by writing the *Logic;* this is to say, the Preface is an introduction to Hegel's system, not simply to the *Phenomenology.*

19. Critical Appraisal of Some Standard Works on
    Hegel's *Phenomenology*

    K. R. Westphal, "Hegel, Idealism, and Robert Pippin," *International Philosophical Quarterly* 33.3 (1993):263–72.

    K. R. Westphal, "Hegel's Epistemology? Reflections on Some Recent Expositions," *Clio* 28.3 (1999):303–23. Critical review article on Klaus Hartmann (various); Joseph Flay, *Hegel's Quest for Certainty;* Robert Pippin, *Hegel's Idealism;* Michael Forster, *Hegel and Skepticism;* Terry Pinkard, *Hegel's Phenomenology: The Sociality of Reason;* and Justus Hartnack, *From Radical Empiricism to Absolute Idealism.*

    P. Reily, "An Introduction to the Reading of Alexandre Kojève," *Political Theory* 9.1 (1981):5–48.

    I. Soll, "Charles Taylor's Hegel," *Journal of Philosophy* (1976); rpt. in M. Inwood, ed., *Hegel* (op. cit.), 54–66.

Bibliography

Allison, Henry, 1983. *Kant's Transcendental Idealism: An Interpretation and Defense.* New Haven: Yale University Press.

———, 1990. *Kant's Theory of Freedom.* Cambridge: Cambridge University Press.

———, 1997. "We Can Act Only under the Idea of Freedom." *Proceedings and Addresses of the American Philosophical Association* 71.2:39–50.

Alston, William P., 1989. *Epistemic Justification.* Ithaca, N.Y.: Cornell University Press.

———, 1994. "Belief-Forming Practices and the Social." In Schmitt, ed., 1994a, 29–51.

Ameriks, Karl, 1978. "Kant's Transcendental Deduction as a Regressive Argument." *Kant-Studien* 69.3:273–87.

Baier, Annette, 1997. *The Commons of the Mind.* LaSalle, Ill.: Open Court.

Baillie, James B., 1901. *The Origin and Significance of Hegel's Logic.* London: Macmillan.

Barnes, Barry, David Bloor, and John Henry, 1996. *Scientific Knowledge: A Sociological Analysis.* Chicago: University of Chicago Press.

Baum, Manfred, 1986. *Deduktion und Beweis in Kants Transzendentalphilosophie.* Könnigstein/Ts.: Hein bei Athenäum.

Bealer, George, 1999. "The *A Priori.*" In *The Blackwell Guide to Epistemology,* eds. J. Greco and E. Sosa, 243–70. Oxford: Blackwell.

Beaumont, Bernard, 1954. "Hegel and the Seven Planets." *Mind* 62:246–8.

Beck, Lewis White, ed. and tr., 1988. *Kant Selections.* New York: Macmillan.

Beiser, Frederick C., 1987. *The Fate of Reason.* Cambridge, Mass.: Harvard University Press.

———, ed., 1993a. *The Cambridge Companion to Hegel.* Cambridge: Cambridge University Press.

———, 1993b. "Hegel's Historicism." In Beiser, ed., 1993a, 270–300.

Biagioli, Mario, ed., 1999. *The Science Studies Reader.* London: Routledge.

Bierce, Ambrose, 1958. *The Devil's Dictionary.* New York: Dover.

Bieri, Peter, 1989. "Scepticism and Intentionality." In *Reading Kant,* eds. E. Schaper and W. Vossenkuhl, 77–113. Oxford: Blackwell.

Blackburn, Simon, 1998. *Ruling Passions.* Oxford: Clarendon Press.

Boghosian, Paul, and Christopher Peacocke, eds., 2000. *New Essays on the A Priori.* Oxford: Clarendon Press.

Bohman, James, 1991. *New Philosophy of Social Science.* Cambridge, Mass.: MIT Press.

Brandom, Robert, 1979. "Freedom and Constraint by Norms." *American Philosophical Quarterly* 16.3:187–96.

———, 1994. *Making It Explicit*. Cambridge, Mass.: Harvard University Press.

———, 1999. "Some Pragmatist Themes in Hegel's Idealism." *European Journal of Philosophy* 7.2:164–89.

Brodbeck, May, 1973. "Methodological Individualisms: Definition and Reduction." In O'Neill, ed., 1973, 287–311.

Burge, Tyler, 1979. "Individualism and the Mental." *Midwest Studies in Philosophy* 4:73–121.

———, 1986. "Intellectual Norms and Foundations of Mind." *Journal of Philosophy* 83.12:697–720.

———, 1992. "Philosophy of Language and Mind: 1950–1990." *Philosophical Review* 101.1:3–51.

Burke, Tom, 1994. *Dewey's New Logic: A Reply to Russell*. Chicago: University of Chicago Press.

Carnap, Rudolf, 1934. *Logischer Syntax der Sprache*. Vienna: Springer. Tr. by A. Smeaton, *The Logical Syntax of Language*. Paterson, N.J.: Littlefield, Adams, & Co., 1959.

———, 1950. "Empiricism, Semantics, and Ontology." *Revue International de Philosophie* 4. Revised version in Carnap, *Meaning and Necessity,* 205–21. Chicago: University of Chicago Press, 1956.

———, 1956. "The Methodological Character of Theoretical Concepts." In *Minnesota Studies in Philosophy of Science,* vol. 1., eds., H. Feigl and M. Scriven, 38–76. Minneapolis: University of Minnesota Press.

Chisholm, Roderick, 1957. *Perceiving: A Philosophical Study*. Ithaca, N.Y.: Cornell University Press.

———, 1973. *The Problem of The Criterion*. Milwaukee: Marquette University Press.

———, 1976. *Person and Object*. LaSalle, Ill.: Open Court.

Clarke, Desmond, 1982. *Descartes' Philosophy of Science*. Manchester: Manchester University Press.

Cling, Andrew, 1994. "Posing the Problem of the Criterion." *Philosophical Studies* 75:261–92.

Coady, C. A. J., 1992. *Testimony: A Philosophical Study*. Oxford: Oxford University Press.

Conant, James, 2002. "The Method of the Tractatus." In *From Frege to Wittgenstein,* ed. E. Reck, 374–462. Oxford: Oxford University Press.

Cooper, John M., 1980. "Aristotle on Friendship." In *Essays on Aristotle's Ethics,* ed. A. Rorty, 301–40. Berkeley: University of California Press.

Dancy, Jonathan, 1985. *Introduction to Contemporary Epistemology*. Oxford: Blackwell.

Davidson, Donald, 1984. *Inquiries into Truth and Interpretation*. New York: Oxford University Press.

―――, 1989. "The Conditions of Thought." In *The Mind of Donald Davidson*, eds. J. Brandl and W. Gombocz. *Grazer Philosophische Studien* 36:193–200.

―――, 1991. "Three Varieties of Knowledge." In *A. J. Ayer: Memorial Essays*, ed. A. P. Griffiths, 153–66. Cambridge: Cambridge University Press.

DeGeorge, Richard, 1983. "Social Reality and Social Relations." *Review of Metaphysics* 37:3–20.

deVries, Willem, 1988. *Hegel's Theory of Mental Activity.* Ithaca, N.Y.: Cornell University Press.

―――, 1991. "The Dialectic of Teleology." *Philosophical Topics* 19.2:51–70.

Dewey, John, 1930. *Individualism Old and New.* New York: Minton Bach.

―――, 1939. *The Theory of Valuation.* Chicago: University of Chicago Press.

―――, 1948. *Reconstruction in Philosophy.* 2nd, rev. ed. Boston: Beacon.

Donnellan, Keith, 1966. "Reference and Definite Descriptions." *Philosophical Review* 75.3:281–304.

Dretske, Frederick I., 1969. *Seeing and Knowing.* Chicago: University of Chicago Press.

―――, 1981. *Knowledge and the Flow of Information.* Cambridge, Mass.: MIT/Bradford Press. Designated "*KFI.*"

―――, 1983. "Précis of *Knowledge and the Flow of Information.*" *Behavioral and Brain Sciences* 6:55–63. Rpt. in *Epistemology Naturalized,* ed. H. Kornblith, 169–87. Cambridge, Mass.: MIT Press, 1985.

―――, 1988. *Explaining Behavior: Reasons in a World of Causes.* Cambridge, Mass.: MIT Press.

―――, 1993. "The Nature of Thought." *Philosophical Studies* 70:185–99.

Düsing, Edith, 1986. *Intersubjektivität und Selbstbewußtsein.* Köln: Dinter.

Einstein, Albert, 2000. *The Expanded Quotable Einstein.* Ed. by A. Calaprice. Princeton: Princeton University Press.

Elgin, Katherine Z., 1999. *Considered Judgment.* Princeton: Princeton University Press.

Evans, Gareth, 1975. "Identity and Predication." *Journal of Philosophy* 72.13: 343–63.

Ferrarin, Alfredo, 2001. *Hegel and Aristotle.* Cambridge: Cambridge University Press.

Ferreira, Phillip, 1999. *Bradley and the Structure of Knowledge.* Albany: SUNY Press.

Ferrini, Cinzia, 1994. "On Newton's Demonstration of Kepler's Second Law in Hegel's *De orbitis planetarum* (1801)." *Philosophia naturalis* 31.1:150–70.

―――, 1995. *Guida al "De orbitis planetarum" di Hegel ed alle sue edizioni e traduzioni.* Bern: Haupt.

―――, 2002. "La dialettica di etica e linguaggio in Hegel interprete dell'eroicità di *Antigone.*" In *Antichi e nuovi dialoghi di sapienti e eroi,* ed. L. M. Napolitano Valditara, 179–243. Trieste: Edizioni Università di Trieste.

———, 2004. "La *Differenzschrift:* modelli di identità e filosofie della natura in Hegel e Schelling." In *L'esordio pubblico di Hegel. Per il bicentenario della Differenzschrift,* ed. M. Cingoli. Milan: Guerini.

Fodor, Jerry, and Ernest LePore, 1992. *Holism: A Shopper's Guide.* Oxford: Blackwell.

Fogelin, Robert, 1994. *Pyrrhonian Reflections on Knowledge and Justification.* Oxford: Oxford University Press.

Gardner, Sebastian, 1999. *Kant and the Critique of Pure Reason.* London: Routledge.

Gettier, Edmund, 1963. "Is Justified True Belief Knowledge?" *Analysis* 23.6: 121–3.

Gilbert, Margaret, 1994. "Remarks on Collective Belief." In Schmitt, ed., 1994a, 235–56.

Goldman, Alvin, 1976. "Discrimination and Perceptual Knowledge." *Journal of Philosophy* 73.20:771–91.

———, 1986. *Epistemology and Cognition.* Cambridge, Mass.: Harvard University Press.

———, 1999. *Knowledge in a Social World.* Oxford: Clarendon Press.

Goldstein, Leon J., 1973. "Two Theses of Methodological Individualism." In O'Neill, ed., 1973, 277–86.

Golinski, Jan, 1998. *Making Natural Knowledge.* Cambridge: Cambridge University Press.

Goodman, Nelson, 1965. *Fact, Fiction, and Forecast.* Indianapolis: Bobbs-Merrill.

Gopnick, Alison, Andrew Meltzoff, and Patricia Kuhl, 1999. *The Scientist in the Crib: Minds, Brains, and How Children Learn.* New York: Morrow.

Green, Thomas, 1999. *Voices: The Educational Formation of Conscience.* South Bend, Ind.: Notre Dame University Press.

Griffin, James, 1996. *Value Judgment: Improving Our Ethical Beliefs.* Oxford: Clarendon Press.

Haack, Susan, 1993. *Evidence and Inquiry.* Oxford: Blackwell.

———, 1998. *Manifesto of a Passionate Moderate.* Chicago: University of Chicago Press.

Hare, Peter, 1998. "Classical Pragmatism, Recent Naturalistic Theories of Representation, and Pragmatic Realism." In *The Role of Pragmatics in Contemporary Philosophy,* eds. P. Weingartner, G. Schurz, and G. Dorn, 58–65. Vienna: Hölder-Pichler-Tempsky.

Harris, H. S., 1997. *Hegel's Ladder,* 2 vols. Indianapolis: Hackett.

Hartnack, Justus, 1998. *An Introduction to Hegel's Logic.* Indianapolis: Hackett.

Hegel, G. W. F., 1968– . *Gesammelte Werke,* eds. H. Buchner and O. Pöggeler. Hamburg: Meiner.

———, [1853] 1974. *Hegel's Ansichten über Erziehung und Unterricht,* 4 vols. Ed. by G. Thaulow. Kiel. Rpt., Glashütten im Taunus: Auvermann.

———, 1980. *Phänomenologie des Geistes*. In *Gesammelte Werke*, vol. 9.

———, 1977. *The Phenomenology of Spirit*. Tr. by A. V. Miller. Oxford: Clarendon Press.

———, 1831. *Encyclopedia of Philosophical Sciences*. (*Enz.*) 3rd ed. In *Gesammelte Werke*, vol. 20.

———, 1991. *The Encyclopedia Logic*. Tr. by T. F. Geraets, W. A. Suchting, and H. S. Harris. Indianapolis: Hackett. (*Enz.* I)

———, 1970. *Hegel's Philosophy of Nature*, 3 vols. Ed. and tr. by M. J. Petry. London: George Allen & Unwin; New York: Humanities Press (*Enz.* II)

———, 1971. *Hegel's Philosophy of Mind*. Tr. by W. Wallace and A. V. Miller. Oxford: Clarendon Press. (*Enz.* III)

———, 1978. *Hegel's Philosophy of Subjective Spirit*, 3 vols. Ed. and tr. by M. J. Petry. Dordrecht: Reidel. (Contains the first half of *Enz.* III; omits Hegel's social philosophy.)

———, 1991. *Elements of the Philosophy of Right*. Ed. by A. W. Wood, and tr. by H. B. Nisbet. Cambridge: Cambridge University Press.

Hookway, Christopher, 1999. "Modest Transcendental Arguments and Sceptical Doubts: A Reply to Stroud." In *Transcendental Arguments: Problems and Prospects,* ed. R. Stern, 173–87. Oxford: Oxford University Press.

Horstmann, Rolf-Peter, 1984. *Ontologie und Relationen*. Könnigstein/Ts.: Anthenäum-Hain.

Hoy, David C., 1989. "Hegel's Critique of Kantian Morality." *History of Philosophy Quarterly* 6.2:207–32.

Hundert, Edward M., 1989. *Philosophy, Psychiatry, and Neuroscience*. Oxford: Clarendon Press.

Hylton, Peter, 1990. *Russell, Idealism, and the Emergence of Analytic Philosophy*. Oxford: Clarendon Press.

Janko, R., 1987. Introduction to *Poetics,* by Aristotle, tr. by R. Janko, ix–xxvi. Indianapolis: Hackett.

Kant, Immanuel, 1902– . *Kritik der reinen Vernunft*. In *idem., Gesammelte Schriften,* vols. 3, 4. Königlich preussische Akademie der Wissenschaften. Berlin: deGruyter.

Kaufmann, Walter, 1965. *Hegel: A Re-Interpretation*. Garden City, N.Y.: Anchor.

Kitcher, Philip, 1992. "The Naturalists Return." *Philosophical Review* 101.1: 53–114.

———, 1994. "Contrasting Conceptions of Social Epistemology." In Schmitt, ed., 1994a, 111–34.

Kolb, David, 1991. "What Is Open and What Is Closed in Hegel's System." *Philosophical Topics* 19.2:29–50.

Kornblith, Hilary, 1994. "A Conservative Approach to Social Epistemology." In Schmitt, ed., 1994a, 93–111.

Kripke, Saul, 1972. "Naming and Necessity." In *Semantics of Natural Language*, eds. D. Davidson and G. Harman, 253–355. Dordrecht: Reidel.

———, 1982. *Wittgenstein on Rules and Private Language.* Oxford: Blackwell.

Kuhn, Thomas, 1977. *The Essential Tension.* Chicago: University of Chicago Press.

Lamb, David, ed., 1998. *Hegel,* 2 vols. Dartmouth: Ashgate.

Lavine, Thelma Z., 1949. "Knowledge as Interpretation: An Historical Survey." *Philosophy and Phenomenological Research* 10 (1949–50):526–40, and 11 (1950–51):88–103.

Lessing, G. E., 1780. *Erziehung des Menschengeschlechts.* Berlin: Voss und Sohn.

Locke, John, 1975. *An Essay Concerning Human Understanding.* Ed. by P. H. Nidditch. Oxford: Clarendon Press.

Longino, Helen E., 1994. "The Fate of Knowledge in Social Theories of Science." In Schmitt, ed., 1994a, 135–57.

Mandelbaum, Maurice, 1973. "Societal Facts." In O'Neill, ed., 1973, 221–47.

McDowell, John, 1994. *Mind and World.* Cambridge, Mass.: Harvard University Press.

———, 1998. "Having the World in View: Sellars, Kant, and Intentionality." *Journal of Philosophy* 95.9:431–91.

———, 1999. "Comments on Robert Brandom's 'Some Pragmatist Themes in Hegel's Idealism'." *European Journal of Philosophy* 7.2:190–3.

Mittelstraß, Jürgen, ed., 1980, 2001. *Enzyklopädie Philosophie und Wissenschaftstheorie.* Stuttgart/Weimar: Metzler.

Moore, Chris, and Philip Dunham, 1995. *Joint Attention: Its Origins and Role in Development.* Mahwah, N.J.: Erlbaum.

Moser, Paul, Dwayne Mulder, and J. D. Trout, 1998. *The Theory of Knowledge: A Thematic Introduction.* New York: Oxford University Press.

Moser, Paul, and Arnold vander Nat, eds., 1995. *Human Knowledge: Classical and Contemporary Approaches.* 2nd ed. New York: Oxford University Press.

Nagel, Ernest, and Richard Brandt, eds., 1965. *Meaning and Knowledge: Systematic Readings in Epistemology.* New York: Harcourt, Brace & World.

Napolitano Valditara, Linda M., 2002. "Scenografie morali nell'*Antigone* e nell'*Edipo re:* Sofocle e Aristotele." In *Antichi e nuovi dialoghi di sapienti ed eroi,* ed. idem., 101–49. Trieste: Edizioni Università di Trieste.

Nasti De Vincentis, Mauro, 1997. "Hegel's Worm in Newton's Apple." In *Hegel and the Philosophy of Nature,* ed. S. Houlgate, 227–56. Albany: SUNY Press.

Neuhouser, Frederick, 1986. "Deducing Desire and Recognition in the *Phenomenology of Spirit.*" *Journal of the History of Philosophy* 24:243–62.

———, 1994. "Fichte and the Relation between Right and Morality." In *Fichte: Historical Context/Contemporary Controversies,* eds. D. Breazeale and T. Rockmore, 158–80. New York: Humanities Press.

———, 2000. *The Foundations of Hegel's Social Theory: Actualizing Freedom.* Cambridge, Mass.: Harvard University Press.

———, 2003. "Rousseau on the Relation between Reason and Self-Love (*Amour propre*)." *Internationales Jarbuch des deutschen Idealismus/International Yearbook of German Idealism* 1:221–39.

Nussbaum, Martha, 1986. *The Fragility of Goodness.* Cambridge: Cambridge University Press. 2nd ed., 2002 (new Foreword; text unrev.).

O'Neill, John, ed., 1973. *Modes of Individualism and Collectivism.* New York: St. Martin's.

O'Neill, Onora, 1992. "Vindicating Reason." In *The Cambridge Companion to Kant,* ed. P. Guyer, 280–308. Cambridge: Cambridge University Press.

———, 2003. "Constructivism in Rawls and Kant." In *The Cambridge Companion to Rawls,* ed. S. Freeman, 347–67. Cambridge: Cambridge University Press.

Ostwald, Martin, 1973. "Was There a Concept of agraphos nomos in Classical Greece?" In *Exegesis and Argument,* eds. E. N. Lee, et al., 70–104. *Phronesis* Supp. Vol. I. Assen: van Gorcum.

Peacocke, Christopher, 1998. "Nonconceptual Content Defended." *Philosophy and Phenomenological Research* 58:381–8.

Peirce, C. S., 1877. "The Fixation of Belief." *CP* (Peirce 1931) 5:358–87; *WCSP* (Peirce 1982) 3:242–57.

———, 1878. "How to Make Our Ideas Clear." *CP* 5:388–410; *WCSP* 3:257–76.

———, 1905. "What Pragmatism Is." *CP* 5, §§411–37.

———, 1931. *Collected Papers.* Ed. by C. Hartshorne, P. Weiss, and A. Burks, Cambridge, Mass.: Harvard University Press, 1931–5, 1958. Designated "*CP.*"

———, 1982. *Writings of Charles S. Peirce: A Chronological Edition,* eds. M. Fisch, et. al., Bloomington: Indiana University Press. Designated "*WCSP.*"

Perlmutter, Martin, 1998. "Moral Intuitions and Philosophical Method." In Westphal, ed., 1998g, 203–18.

Pettit, Philip, 1996. *Common Mind: An Essay on Psychology, Society, and Politics.* Oxford: Oxford University Press.

Phillips, D. C., 1976. *Holistic Thought in Social Science.* Stanford: Stanford University Press.

Pinker, Steven, 1994. *The Language Instinct.* New York: William Morrow.

Plantinga, Alvin, 1993. *Warrant and Proper Function.* New York: Oxford University Press.

Pollock, John, 1986. *Contemporary Theories of Knowledge.* Lanham, Md.: Rowman & Littlefield.

———, and Joseph Cruz, 1999. *Contemporary Theories of Knowledge.* Rev. ed. Lanham, Md.: Rowman & Littlefield.

Price, H. H., 1932. *Perception.* London: Methuen.

Putnam, Hilary, 1975–6. "What Is Realism?" *Proceedings of the Aristotelian Society* 76:177–94.

———, 1977. "Realism and Reason." *Proceeding and Addresses of the American Philosophical Association* 50 (1976–7). Rpt. in *idem., Meaning and the Moral Sciences,* 123–40. London: Routledge & Kegan Paul.

———, 1980. "Models and Reality." *Journal of Symbolic Logic* 45.3:464–82.

———, 1981. *Reason, Truth, and History.* Cambridge, Mass.: Harvard University Press.

Quine, W. V. O., 1951. "Two Dogmas of Empiricism." Rpt. in Quine (1961), 20–46.

———, 1953. *From a Logical Point of View.* Cambridge, Mass.: Harvard University Press.

———, 1960. *Word and Object.* Cambridge, Mass.: MIT Press.

———, 1961. *From a Logical Point of View.* 2nd, rev. ed. (1st ed., 1953). Cambridge, Mass.: Harvard University Press.

———, 1969. *Ontological Relativity and Other Essays.* New York: Columbia University Press.

———, 1975. *The Roots of Reference.* LaSalle, Ill.: Open Court.

———, 1995. *From Stimulus to Science.* Cambridge, Mass.: Harvard University Press.

Rauch, Leo, and David Sherman, 1999. *Hegel's Phenomenology of Self-Consciousness.* Albany: SUNY Press.

Rawls, John, 1971. *A Theory of Justice.* Cambridge, Mass.: Harvard University Press.

Reidy, David, 1999. "Rawls's Idea(l) of Public Reason." *Polis* 6:93–113.

———, 2000. "Rawls's Wide View of Public Reason: Not Wide Enough." *Res Publica* 6:1–25.

Ritter, J., and K. Gründer, eds., 1971. *Historisches Wörterbuch der Philosophie.* Basel: Schwabe.

Robinson, Jonathan, 1977. *Duty and Hypocrisy in Hegel's Phenomenology of Mind.* Toronto: University of Toronto Press.

Root, Michael, 1998. "How to Teach a Wise Man." In Westphal, ed., 1998g, 89–110.

Rorty, Richard, 1970. "Strawson's Objectivity Argument." *Review of Metaphysics* 24:207–44.

———, 1971. "Verificationism and Transcendental Arguments." *Nous* 5:3–14.

———, 1972. "The World Well Lost." *Journal of Philosophy* 69:649–65. Rpt. in *Consequences of Pragmatism,* 3–18. Minneapolis: University of Minnesota Press, 1982.

———, 1979. *Philosophy and the Mirror of Nature.* Princeton: Princeton University Press.

Rosenkranz, Sven, 2001. "Farewell to Objectivity: A Critique of Brandom." *Philosophical Quarterly* 51.203:232–7.

Roskies, Adina, guest ed., 1999. "The Binding Problem." *Neuron* 24:7–125.

Rouse, Joseph, 2002. *How Scientific Practices Matter.* Chicago: University of Chicago Press.

Russell, Bertrand, 1914. *Our Knowledge of the External World.* London: George Allen & Unwin.

———, 1994. *The Collected Papers of Bertrand Russell,* J. Passmore, general ed. London: Routledge. Designated "*CP.*"

Sandkühler, H. J., ed., 1990. *Europäische Enzyklopädie zu Philosophie und Wissenschaften.* Hamburg: Meiner.

Savigny, Eike von, 1991. "Self-Conscious Individual versus Social Self: The Rationale of Wittgenstein's Discussion of Rule Following." *Philosophy and Phenomenological Research* 51:67–84.

Scharff, Robert, 1995. *Compte after Positivism.* Cambridge: Cambridge University Press.

Schelling, F. W. J., 1800. "Allgemeine Deduktion des dynamischen Processes oder der Kategorien der Physik." In *Schellings Werke,* ed. M. Schrötter, 2:637–712. Munich: Beck & Oldenbourg, 1927.

Schmitt, Frederick, 1987. "Justification, Sociality, and Autonomy." *Synthese* 73.1:43–85.

———, ed., 1994a. *Socializing Epistemology.* Lanham, Md.: Rowman & Littlefield.

———, 1994b. "The Justification of Group Beliefs." In Schmitt, ed., 1994a, 257–87.

Sellars, Wilfrid, 1947. "Pure Pragmatics and Epistemology." *Philosophy of Science* 15.3:181–202.

———, 1948. "Concepts as Involving Laws and as Inconceivable without Them." *Philosophy of Science* 15.4:287–315.

———, 1963a. *Science, Perception, and Reality.* London: Routledge.

———, 1963b. "Empiricism and the Philosophy of Mind." In Sellars 1963a, 127–96.

———, 1968. *Science and Metaphysics.* London: Routledge.

———, 1981. "Mental Events." *Philosophical Studies* 39:325–45.

———, 1989. *The Metaphysics of Epistemology.* Atascadero, Calif.: Ridgeview.

Sextus Empiricus, 1933. *Outlines of Pyrrhonism.* Tr. by Rev. R. G. Bury. Loeb Library. Cambridge, Mass.: Harvard University Press. Designated as "*PH.*"

Shook, John, ed., 2003. *Pragmatic Naturalism and Realism.* Buffalo, N.Y.: Prometheus.

Solomon, Miriam, 1994a. "Social Empiricism." *Nous* 28.3:325–43.

———, 1994b. "A More Social Epistemology." In Schmitt, ed., 1994a, 217–33.

Sophocles, 1962. *Antigone,* directed by G. Tzavella. © 1962, I W Films, Inc. Reissued by Hen's Tooth Video, 1989. (1124 S. Solano; Las Cruces, NM 88001.)

———, 2001. *Antigone.* Ed. and tr. by P. Woodruff. Indianapolis: Hackett.

Sosa, Ernest, 1991. *Knowledge in Perspective*. Cambridge: Cambridge University Press.

Steinhauer, Kurt, and Gitta Hausen, eds., 1980. *Hegel: Bibliography—Bibliographie*. Munich: K. G. Saur.

Stekeler-Weithofer, Pirmin, 1992. *Hegels Analytische Philosophie. Die Wissenschaft der Logik als kritische Theorie der Bedeutung*. Paderborn: Schöningh.

Stern, Robert, ed., 1993. *G. W. F. Hegel: Critical Assessments*, 4 vols. London: Routledge.

Strawson, Peter F., 1959. *Individuals*. London: Methuen.

———, 1966. *The Bounds of Sense*. London: Methuen.

———, 1974. *Subject and Predicate in Logic and Grammar*. London: Methuen.

Stroud, Barry, 1984. "The Allure of Idealism." *Proceedings of the Aristotelian Society* Supplement 58:243–58.

———, 1999. "The Goal of Transcendental Arguments." In *Transcendental Arguments: Problems and Prospects*, ed. R. Stern, 155–72. Oxford: Oxford University Press.

Thucydides, 1998. *The Peloponnesian War*. Tr. by S. Lattimore. Indianapolis: Hackett.

Tye, Michael, 1995. *Ten Problems of Consciousness*. Cambridge, Mass.: MIT Press.

Weiss, Frederick, ed., 1974. *Beyond Epistemology*. The Hague: Nijhoff.

Westphal, Kenneth R., 1989a. *Hegel's Epistemological Realism*. Philosophical Studies Series, vol. 43. Dordrecht: Kluwer.

———, 1989b. "Hegel's Attitude toward Jacobi in the 'Third Attitude of Thought toward Objectivity'." *Southern Journal of Philosophy* 27.1:135–56.

———, 1991. "Hegel's Critique of Kant's Moral World View." *Philosophical Topics* 19.2:133–76.

———, 1992. "Hegel." In *A Companion to Epistemology*, eds. E. Sosa and J. Dancy, 167–70. Oxford: Blackwell.

———, 1993. "The Basic Context and Structure of Hegel's *Philosophy of Right*." In Beiser, ed., 1993a, 234–69.

———, 1994. "Community as the Basis of Free Individual Action." In *Communitarianism*, ed. M. Daly, 36–40. Belmont, Calif.: Wadsworth. (Annotated translations from Hegel's *Phenomenology*.)

———, 1995. "How 'Full' is Kant's Categorical Imperative?" *Jahrbuch für Recht und Ethik/Annual Review of Law and Ethics* 3:465–509.

———, 1996. "Kant, Hegel, and the Transcendental Material Conditions of Possible Experience." *Bulletin of the Hegel Society of Great Britain* 33:23–41.

———, 1997a. "Affinity, Idealism, and Naturalism: The Stability of Cinnabar and the Possibility of Experience." *Kant-Studien* 88:139–89.

———, 1997b. "Hegel, Philosophy, and Mathematical Physics." *Bulletin of the Hegel Society of Great Britain* 36:1–15.

———, 1998a. *Hegel, Hume und die Identität wahrnehmbarer Dinge.* Frankfurt am Main: Klostermann.

———, 1998b. "Hegel's Solution to the Dilemma of the Criterion." Revised version in *The Phenomenology of Spirit Reader: A Collection of Critical and Interpretive Essays,* ed. J. Stewart, 76–91. Albany: SUNY Press.

———, 1998c. "Harris, Hegel, and the Spirit of the *Phenomenology.*" *Clio* 27.4:551–72.

———, 1998d. "Hegel and Hume on Perception and Concept-Empiricism." *Journal of the History of Philosophy* 33:99–123.

———, 1998e. "Transcendental Reflections on Pragmatic Realism." In Westphal, ed., 1998g, 17–59.

———, 1998f. "On Hegel's Early Critique of Kant's *Metaphysical Foundations of Natural Science.*" In *Hegel and the Philosophy of Nature,* ed. S. Houlgate, 137–66. Albany: SUNY Press.

———, ed., 1998g. *Pragmatism, Reason, & Norms.* New York: Fordham University Press.

———, 1999, "Hegel's Epistemology? Reflections on Some Recent Expositions." *Clio* 28.3:303–23.

———, 2000a. "Hegel's Internal Critique of Naïve Realism." *Journal of Philosophical Research* 25:173–229.

———, 2000b. "Hegel, Harris, and Sextus Empiricus." *Owl of Minerva* 31.2: 155–72.

———, 2000c. "Is Hegel's *Phenomenology* Relevant to Contemporary Epistemology?" *Bulletin of the Hegel Society of Great Britain* 41/42:43–85.

———, 2002a. "Hegel's Standards of Political Legitimacy." *Jahrbuch für Recht und Ethik/Annual Review of Law and Ethics* 10 (2002):307–30.

———, 2002b. "Kant, Hegel, and the Fate of 'the' Intuitive Intellect." In *The Reception of Kant's Critical Philosophy: Fichte, Schelling, and Hegel,* ed. S. Sedgwick, 283–305. New York: Cambridge University Press.

———, 2002c. "L'ispirazione tragica della dialettica fenomenologica di Hegel." In *Antichi e nuovi dialoghi di sapienti e eroi,* ed. L. M. Napolitano Valditara, 151–77. Trieste: Edizioni Università di Trieste.

———, 2003a. "Hegel's Manifold Response to Scepticism in the Phenomenology of Spirit." *Proceedings of the Aristotelian Society* 103.2:149–78.

———, 2003b. "Can Pragmatic Realists Argue Transcendentally?" In *Pragmatic Naturalism and Realism,* ed. J. Shook, 151–75. Buffalo, N.Y.: Prometheus.

———, 2003c. "Epistemic Reflection and Cognitive Reference in Kant's Transcendental Response to Skepticism." *Kant-Studien* 94.2:135–71.

———, 2003d. "Objektive Gültigkeit zwischen Gegebenem und Gemachtem. Hegels kantischer Konstruktivismus in der praktischen Philosophie." *Jahrbuch für Recht und Ethik/Annual Review of Law and Ethics* 11.

———, 2004. "'Sense Certainty,' or Why Russell Had No 'Knowledge by Acquaintance'." *Bulletin of the Hegel Society of Great Britain*, 47/48.

Wettstein, Howard, 1991. *Has Semantics Rested on a Mistake?* Stanford: Stanford University Press.

Wick, Warner, 1951. "The 'Political' Philosophy of Logical Empiricism." *Philosophical Studies* 2.4:49–57.

Will, Frederick L., 1974. *Induction and Justification*. Ithaca, N.Y.: Cornell University Press.

———, 1988. *Beyond Deduction*. London: Routledge.

———, 1997. *Pragmatism and Realism*. Ed. by K. R. Westphal. Lanham, Md.: Rowman & Littlefield.

Williams, Robert, 1998. *Hegel's Ethics of Recognition*. Berkeley: University of California Press.

Wilson, Margaret, 1992. "History of Philosophy Today; and the Case of Sensible Qualities." *Philosophical Review* 101.1:191–243.

———, 1999. *Ideas and Mechanism*. Princeton: Princeton University Press.

Wolff, Michael, 1992. *Das Körper-Seele-Problem*. Frankfurt am Main: Klostermann.

Wright, Crispin, 1986. "Does *Philosophical Investigations* I.258–60 Suggest a Cogent Argument against Private Language?" In *Subject, Thought, and Context*, eds. P. Pettit and J. McDowell, 209–66. Oxford: Clarendon Press.

———, 1992. *Truth and Objectivity*. Cambridge, Mass.: Harvard University Press.

Name Index

Agrippa, 9, 9n1, 32
Alston, William, 92n1, 99, 105
Antigone, 17–9, 21, 22, 22n11, 24–5, 27, 28n17, 30, 31, 31n6
Aristotle, 1, 7, 29, 31n4, 33, 55, 62n15, 97, cf. 90
Ayer, A. J., 73n1, 101

Berkeley, Bishop George, 36n12, 59
Bierce, Ambrose, 38
Bieri, Peter, 96n5
Blackburn, Simon, 82
Bradley, F. H., 89
Brandom, Robert, 53n3, 62–3n15, 65n17, 99n7
Burge, Tyler, 76, 77–8, 103, 103n1, 107
Burke, Thomas, 89

Carnap, Rudolf, 9, 48–9, 63n15, 71, 74n3, 75, 82, 83, 92, 101, 103n2
Chisholm, Roderick, 2, 84
Comte, August, 89
Conant, James, 9
Creon, 3, 14–28, 31, 31n6, 32–4
Crusoe, Robinson, 105n8, 106

Davidson, Donald, 42, 43n5, 60, 96n5
Descartes, René, 78, 87n7, 88, 92n1, 103
Dewey, John, 49, 73, 89, 114n20
Donnellan, Keith, 77
Dretske, Frederick, 3, 92–100

Einstein, Albert, 47, 108
Eurydice, 22n11, 26
Evans, Gareth, 82n1

Ferreira, Phillip, 89
Feyerabend, Paul, 48
Fichte, J. G., 61
Frege, Gottlob, 8–9, 56

Gettier, Edmund, 105n8
Gilbert, Margaret, 113–4
Goldman, Alvin, 96, 106n9
Goodman, Nelson, 48, 101
Green, T. H., 115n22
Green, Thomas, 78
Griffin, James, 6, 101n11

Haack, Susan, 77, 98n6
Haemon, 19–22, 22n11, 23, 24, 25, 27, 30
Harris, Henry, 5, 57n8, 64n16, 81n11
Hempel, Carl, 73n1, 101, 103n2
Herder, J. G., 88, 98n6, 107
Hookway, Christopher, 57
Horstmann, Rolf-Peter, 115n21
Hume, David, 1, 56, 82, 83n2, 84–5, 84–5n3, 92n1, 103
Hylton, Peter, 89

James, William, 49
Johnson, Dr. Samuel, 36n12

Kant, Immanuel, 4n7, 7–8, 11, 12, 43n5, 54, 56, 59, 62, 64, 65, 68–71, 79–80, 81n12, 83, 85, 85n3, 88, 88n9, 89, 92, 100, 100n9
Kitcher, Philip, 104nn4–6, 110n15, 113n19
Kripke, Saul, 77, 107n9
Kuhn, Thomas, 48, 75, 90

Lessing, G. E., 77
Lewis, C. I., 73n1
Locke, John, 54
Longino, Helen, 112n17
Lorentz, Hendrick, 108

McDowell, John, 43n5, 65n17, 73, 77n6, 80, 90

137

Meitner, Lisa, 108n12
Moser, Paul, 73n2

Neurath, Otto, 73n1, 83, 103n2
Newton, Sir Isaac, 8, 55n5
Nietzsche, Friedrich, 89
Nussbaum, Martha, 14n2, 19, 24n14, 26, 29–30, 31, 31n6, 38

Ockham, William of, 47

Peacocke, Christopher, 42, 43n5
Peirce, Charles Saunders, 49, 64, 69, 73, 78, 114n20
Phillips, D. C., 110–2
Pinker, Steven, 109n13
Plantinga, Alvin, 96
Plato, 87n6
Pollock, John, 87
Polynices, 15, 17, 19, 21n9, 22n11, 23, 24, 26, 27
Popper, Karl, 88
Price, H. H., 77n7, 86n6
Protagoras, 54
Putnam, Hilary, 54, 71, 78, 92, 106

Quine, W. V. O., 54n4, 63n15, 77n7, 82, 84, 84n3, 103n2

Rawls, John, 101
Reichenbach, Hans, 73n1
Robinson, Jonathan, 7
Rorty, Richard, 48, 63n15, 69n20, 90, 97–8n6, 99n7

Rousseau, Jean-Jacques, 10
Russell, Bertrand, 1, 73n1, 75, 82, 84, 85, 85n4, 89

Scharff, Robert, 89
Schelling, F. W. J., 52, 52n2
Schiller, F. C. S., 89
Schlick, Moritz, 73n1
Schmitt, James, 113–4
Sellars, Wilfrid, 49, 63n15, 64, 65n17, 77n7, 80, 87n6, 97n6
Sextus Empiricus, 2, 38–9, 48, 50, 54n4, 89, 98
Sophocles, 3, 14, 15, 15n6, 27, 28, 29, 34
Sosa, Ernest, 87–8
Strawson, Sir Peter F., 60, 74, 74n4, 86–7n5, 88, 88n9
Stroud, Barry, 76

Tiresias, 22n11, 23–4
Tye, Michael, 42, 43n5

Waismann, Friedrich, 73n1
Wettstein, Howard, 77
Wick, Warner, 101
Will, Frederick L., 38, 63n15, 73, 77n6, 81n13, 89, 114–5n20
Wilson, Margaret, 89–90
Wittgenstein, Ludwig, 50, 60, 61, 81n12, 85, 97n6, 107n9
Wright, Crispin, 61n14, 71

Subject Index

absolute, the (Hegel), *defined,* 8
Absolute Knowing (*PhdG*), 62, 64
adequacy, interpretive, standards of, xi, 5
affect, *see* intellect and affect
affinity, transcendental, 57, 65–71, 87; *defined,* 65, 68
alternative, neglected (Kant), 70
alternatives, relevant, *see* justification, relevant alternatives
analysis, transcendental (Kant), 12
ancestors, intellectual, 90; *also see* norms, conventional; reason vs. tradition
Animal Kingdom of the Spirit (*PhdG*), 62n15
animals, 94, 97
anti-Cartesianism, 4, 76, 103; *also see* externalism, mental-content; Cartesianism
Antigone, 3, 14–31, 33; Hegel's analysis of, 14n2, 28n17, 31n6
anti-individualism (Burge), *defined,* 78, 103n1; *also see* anti-Cartesianism; externalism, mental-content
a priori–a posteriori distinction, 57
argument, proof, 10–11, 31; *defined,* 11; sound, *defined,* 11; valid, *defined,* 10–11; transcendental, 11, 56–7, 88n9, consistent with pragmatism, 88–9n10
assessment, mutual critical, *see* criticism, mutual
atomistic individualism, *see* individualism, substantive
Aufhebung, defined, 16
autonomy, 34–5, 79–80; *defined,* 79–80
awe-ful, *see deinon*

ball throwing, *see* throwing ball
Begriff (Hegel), 9, 53–4
binding problem, *defined,* 85–6

Cartesian, Cartesianism, 75, 76, 77, 78; *also see* anti-Cartesianism
catharsis (Aristotle), 33–4
cause, conception of, 59; causal characteristics, 53; causal force, 54–5
causes and norms, *see* norms, and causes
caveats, 5
certainty, epistemic, 8, 72, 76; form of consciousness', 8, 16, 17, 20, 21, 33, 61
chaos, transcendental, *defined,* 69
circularity, justificatory, *see* justification, circular; vicious, 36, 45, 48, 50
classification, 52, 54, 59, 63–4, 68–71, 98, 99n7; *also see* affinity, identification, particulars
cognitive capacities, inventory of, 11, cf. 69, 105–6; *also see* mind, philosophy of
cognitive development, *see* knowledge, cognitive development; education
coherentism, *see* justification, coherence theories of
cold war, 115
collectivism, moderate, 107–14; *defined,* 107, 111; consistent with methodological individualism, 110; in epistemology, 2, 103–15, ; *also see* knowledge, social and historical account of
commitment, undertaking, 34–5
concept-empiricism, 4, 51, 58, 82, 83, 84, 87, 87n7, 88; *defined,* 58
conception, *defined,* 9; empirical, 43, 69, 84, 95, *defined broadly,*

conception (*continued*)
83 (*also see* concept-empiricism);
observation terms, 45, 51; simple,
formation of, 95–6; vs.
concept (*Begriff*), 9, 55
conceptions, native, 83n2; pure a
priori, 43, 43n5, 58, 82–4, 88, 95,
listed, 82, cf. 86n6
conceptual scheme, *see* scheme,
conceptual
conditions, enabling, 108
Conscience (*PhdG*), 62, 63–4
consciousness, forms of (*PhdG*), 3,
8, 9; certainty of, *see* certainty;
assessment of, 36–7; closure of
series, 46n7; Creon as, 14–7;
defined, 9–10, 36, 40; of an object,
six aspects of, 40; self-critical
structure of, 4, 9, 36, 40–4, 98;
series of, 37, 45, 46, 46n7, 50, 58,
66; three phases of, 16
conservatism, 77
constructivism, 73, 77, 78–9;
defined, 73
content, mental, narrow, *defined*, 78;
semantic, 43; *also see* meaning;
externalism, semantic; reference,
descriptions theory of
context, of assertion, action,
assessment, 98
conventions, *see* norms,
conventional
corporate epistemology, *see*
epistemology, corporate
creation ex nihilo, 108
creativity, *see* innovation
Criterion, Dilemma of (Sextus
Empiricus), 2, 3, 9, 32, 36, 45,
48, 50, 71, 74, 75, 96, 98; *stated*,
38–9; Hegel's solution to, 38–50
criticism, mutual, 11, 39, 45, 47, 49,
50, 54, 62, 77–9, 81, 90, 95, 96,
98–101, 108, 112, 114n20
critique, internal, 7, 9, 14, 16–7, 35,
45, 46, 57–8, 70, 77–9, 90, 92; of
Creon's views, 17–28

Crusoe cases, 105n8, 106
cultural circle, 101, 103n2
cultural history, *see* history
customs, *see* norms, conventional

deduction, subjective (Kant),
defined, 60
defeaters, justificatory, *see*
justification, defeaters
deinon (awe-ful), *defined*, 24n14
descriptions, definite (Russell),
85n4; *also see* reference,
descriptions theory of
determinate negation, *see* negation,
determinate
determinism, social, 108; *also see*
holism, social
development, cognitive, *see*
knowledge, cognitive
development
dialectic, principles and practices, 7;
phenomenological, 12; *also see*
method, phenomenological
Dilemma of the Criterion, *see*
Criterion, Dilemma of
dogmatism, 35, 36, 45
dualism, mind-body, 52

edict, rule by, 27, 28n17
education (learning, training),
77–81, 94–8, 104–6, 109, 112,
114; as acquisition of norms,
78–81; *also see* judgment,
mature; language, acquisition;
skills
ego-centric predicament, *see*
predicament, ego-centric; sense
data
electrodynamics, 108
empiricism, 80, 87, 87n7; logical,
82; twentieth-century, 3, 4, 74n4,
82–91; liberalization of, 87–8;
verification, 56; *also see* concept-empiricism
enabling conditions, *see* conditions,
enabling

Enlightenment, the, 4, 38, 39, 64, 72, 73, 77, 90–1
Enquiry Concerning Human Understanding (Hume), 84n3
epistemological argument, Hegel's, chart of, 65, 66–7
epistemology, contemporary, 3, 71, *also see* empiricism, twentieth-century; corporate, 114; information theoretic (Dretske), 3, 92–100, vs. causal reliability theory, 93; Hegel's timeliness of, 2, 71, 88, 90–1, *also see* epistemological argument, Hegel's, chart of; justification of an, 44, 92; *also see* method, phenomenological, second-order nature of
equilibrium, reflective, *see* reflective equilibrium
etiquette, 106
Evil and Foregiveness (*PhdG*), 62
experience, basis of, 10, 40, 74–5, cf. 69; elementary sensory, 51, 83; matter of, 65; *also see* affinity
explanation, hypothetico-deductive model of, 54
externalism, *defined*, 4n7; epistemic, 41–2, 45, 46, 100, 100n8, *defined*, 41n4, 99; justificatory, *see* externalism, epistemic; Kant, 4n7; mental-content, 45, 57, 59, 65, 92, 96, 98, 100–1, *defined*, 76; semantic, 45, 52, 71, 75–7, 98, *defined*, 76

fallibilism, 4, 31, 32, 44–50, 51, 54, 62, 81, 92; *defined*, 45–6; and social aspects of knowledge, 81, 95–7
fascism, 115n22
force, *see* cause
Force and Understanding (*PhdG*), 58–9
formal condition (Kant), *defined*, 68

foundationalism, *see* justification, foundationalist
foundherentism (Haack), 77
frameworks, linguistic (Carnap), *see* scheme, conceptual
freedom, 79; *also see* autonomy, innovation, spontaneity
Freedom of Self-Consciousness (*PhdG*), 59
functionalism, 52, 53, 55; *also see* mind, philosophy of

God, 61, 64

hermeneutical tradition, 89
historicism, *see* relativism, historicist
history, 5, 34, 53, 54, 80–1, 88–91; *also see* philosophy, and history
holism, ontological, 53; semantic, 75, 101; social, 102, 103, 107, 108, 111–5; Holism I, II, III (Phillips), *defined*, 111–2
Hollywood movie sets, 94
hypothesis of science, the, *see* science, the hypothesis of

idea (Hegel), *defined*, 54
ideal (Hegel), *defined*, 54
idealism, dogmatic (Berkeley), 59; Hegel's, *defined*, 53; transcendental (Kant), 12, 57, 59–60, 65, 71, 92, *defined*, 70
identification, requires discrimination, 43, 93, 96, cf. 100; *also see* binding problem; particulars, spatio-temporal, identifying
identity, conception of, 52n2, 58, 85–7; conditions, 53; 'is' of (Russell), 1
Immediate Spirit (*PhdG*), 62
incorporation thesis (Kant), 80n10
incorrigibility, *see* certainty, epistemic

individualism, in epistemology, 2, 4, 72–3, 77–9, 90, 92–102, 103–15; in philosophy of mind, *see* mind, philosophy of; liberal, 115n22; methodological, 103–15, *defined,* 103; substantive, 103–7, 109–10, *defined,* 103
indubitability, *see* certainty, epistemic
infants (human), 94; *also see* education; knowledge, cognitive development
information, background, *see* knowledge, background; channels, 93, 94–100, *defined,* 93, social dimensions of, 95–9, 104–5, cf. 109, 112; decoding of, 95–100; digitalized, 94–5n3, 100; intensionality of, 94–5n3; source, *defined,* 93; theory (Dretske), *see* epistemology, information theoretic
inheritance, intellectual, 90, 97, 100; *also see* education; norms, conventional
innovation, 97, 105, 106, 107, 108
instinct, language, *see* language
intellect and affect, integration of, 33–5; *also see* catharsis; self-understanding
intensional opacity, *see* opacity, intensional
intentionality (object-directedness), 95n3
internalism, justificatory, *see* justification, internalist; semantic, 4; mental content, 4; *also see* Cartesianism; individualism; mind, philosophy of
intuitions, philosophical, 101
"I think," 62

judgment, mature, 4, 45, 47–8, 50, 62, 80–1, 100, cf. 97; reflective, 3, 29–37, 47, 69, required for assessing arguments, 30–5; rule-following model of, 29–31, *also see* justification, deductive model of
justification, basing relations, 49, 62, 79–80, 80n9, 81; by inference, 38, 39; circular, 38–9, 45, 48; coherence theories of, 45, 49, 50, 51, 72, 73–5, *defined,* 49; contextual, 51, 100, *defined,* 99; criteria of, 38, 49–50, 54, 92, 98; deductive model of, 38, 39, 48–50; defeaters, 41–3, 45, *also see* fallibilism; externalist, 51; fallible, *see* fallibilism; foundationalist, 51, 72, 73, 88, 99, *defined,* 49; full, 51; infallibilist, 44, 46, 51, 72; internalist, 4, 51, 99; natural scientific, 52–3; of first premises, 38, 48, 50, *also see* self-evidence; principles, substantive; pragmatic, 32, 47–50, 81, cf. 34–5, *also see* knowledge, social and historical account of; rational, 3, 29–31, 31n6, 33–5, *also see* justification, pragmatic; relevant alternatives, elimination of, 92, 93–4, 100, *also see* critique, internal; reliabilist, 41–3, 51, 85, 99; cf. 79, 93–4, 96–100, 100n8; *also see* regress argument; Criterion, Dilemma of; self-evidence, insufficiency of

Kantianism, analytic, 59, 60, 88, 88n9
knowing that, 94; *also see* knowledge, propositional form of
knowledge, aconceptual, 41, 42, 45, 51, 58, 72–3, 75–6, 82, cf. 86n6; active model of, *see* knowledge, passive ideal of, *and* social and historical account of; apparent (putative), 8, 32, 39; background, 93, 95, 96; basic vs. derived, *defined,* 49, 72–3; by

acquaintance, *see* knowledge, aconceptual; causal-reliability theory of, 96, 99; cognitive development, 105n8, 106; first acquisition of, 95, 104, *also see* knowledge, aconceptual; individualist analyses of, 103–15; information theoretic definition of, 95; passive ideal of, 58, 59, 72–3; propositional form of, 94, 96, 100, cf. 97, *also see* "I think"; recursive definition of, 95; social and historical account of, 60, 63, 72, 77–81, 89–91, 92–100, 104–15; sociology of, 48, 107n10; truth condition of, 46

Kultur-Kritik, see history

language, acquisition, 94, 95–7; instinct, 109n13
law, case law model, 63n15; natural (nomological), 51–5, 59, phenomenological account of, *defined*, 54; natural (normative), 18n8, 28n17, 31n6; positive (statutory), 31n6
learning, *see* education
linguistic frameworks (Carnap), *see* scheme, conceptual
logic, formal, 11, 31, 38, 51, 55, 58, 63, 82, 89; *also see* argument
Logic (Hegel), 51, 54, 55
logical constructions (Russell), *see* sense data
logical empiricism, *see* empiricism, logical
Lord and Bondsman (*PhdG*), 61
Lorentz equations, 108

materialism, eliminative, 52; *also see* naturalism
meaning, as use, 50; of terms, defined contextually, 9, defined inferentially (Carnap), 9, cf. 95n3, definite only within a sentence (Frege), 8–9

Metaphysical Foundations of Natural Science (Kant), 7–8
method, phenomenological (Hegel), 3, 7–37, 57; constraints on, 35, 36; literary model for, 14–37; second-order nature of, 35–6, 44; seven key features of, 12–3; *also see* observers, phenomenological
mind, philosophy of, 4, 52, 55–6, 103, 103n1; cognitive capacities 56–7, 69; individualism vs. anti-individualism, 76, 77–9, 89–91; anti-individualism (Burge), *defined*, 78, 103
modernity, 34; *also see* Enlightenment
modes of speech, *see* speech, modes of
moral philosophy, 5, 31n6, 33, 62, 64; *also see* law, natural (normative); reflective equilibrium
movie sets, Hollywood, *see* Hollywood movie sets
Müller-Lyer illusion, 106
multiperspectivalism, philosophical, 5–6
mutual criticism, *see* criticism, mutual; recognition, *see* recognition, mutual

nativism, *see* conceptions, native
naturalism, 52–3, 55, 63, 99n7, 105n8; causal, 56; nonreductive, 64n16, 70, 109
needs, biological, 52, 59, 109
negation, determinate (Hegel), 46, 53n3, 54, 92; *also see* critique, internal
neglected alternative, *see* alternative, neglected
norms, and causes, 79, 81, 85, 104; conventional, 31n6, 63, 77–9, cf. 90

obedience, right or wrong (Creon), 20–1, 23n12, 24, 27
observation terms, *see* conception, concept-empiricism
observers, phenomenological (*PhdG*), 3, 10, 12, 32–3, 50; *also see* method, phenomenological
Observing Nature (*PhdG*), 63
Observing Reason (*PhdG*), 63, 76
Ockham's razor, 47
Of Scepticism with regard to the senses (Hume), 1, 84n3
ontology, social, 102, 103–15; *also see* individualism; holism, social; collectivism, moderate
opacity, intensional, 94–5n3

particularism, 31n4
particulars, identity conditions of, interdependent, 53–4; spatio-temporal, identifying, 43, 45, 51, 58, 68–71, 83–7, 94, 95, 100, *also see* identification
perception, 94, 96, 99, 106, information theoretic vs. causal theory of, 93; neurophysiology of, 42, 85–6, 94, 97, 99n7, 100, 100n8, 109; perceptual synthesis, 85–7, cf. 106, *also see* binding problem; social aspect of, 106
Perception (*PhdG*), 1, 45, 58, 82, 84, 93, cf. 85–7
perceptual synthesis, *see* perception
person-predicates (Strawson), 60
phenomena, social, 53, 54, 63, 77–81
phenomenalism, 58n10, 83, 85, 103
Phenomenology of Spirit (*PhdG*), epistemology central in, 2; epistemological argument in, 51–71; expository structure of, 3, 5, 10, 12, 14–37, 44–5; readers of, difficulties facing, 1–2, 3, 9; table of contents, chart of, 66
philosophical psychology, *see* mind, philosophy of

philosophy, and history, 89–91; rooted in natural science, 52
Philosophy of Nature (Hegel), 52, 54, 55
Philosophy of Spirit (Hegel), 55
Phrenology (*PhdG*), 63
physicalism, 83–4; *also see* naturalism
physical object, 84; conception of, 84–7, *also see* particulars
Physiognomy (*PhdG*), 63
planets, orbits of, 8, 55n5
plural subject, *see* subject, plural
points of view, in *PhdG*, 3, 10, 33, 57; *also see* method, phenomenological; observers, phenomenological
positivism, logical, 48, 101; *also see* Vienna Circle
practitioners, social, 107, cf. 109; *also see* education; knowledge, social and historical account of; judgment, mature; skills
pragmatism, *defined,* 49; American, 46, 49, 114
predicament, ego-centric, 103
predication, 45; 'is' of, 1; *also see* particulars, spatio-temporal, identifying
Preface (*PhdG*), 80, 123n2
premises, substantive, *see* principles, substantive
principles, substantive, 11, 32, 56–7, 98–9; *also see* self-evidence
private language argument (Wittgenstein), 60, 61
proof, *see* argument
proper functioning, see justification, reliabilist
protocol sentence, 101; *also see* conception, empirical; conception, observation terms
Psychology (*PhdG*), 63
psychology, philosophical, *see* mind, philosophy of

question-begging (*petitio principii*), 9, 35–6, 45, 48, 89
rationalism, 51, 52, 84, 87, 87n7, 88; mad, 35n11, 52, 52n7
rationality, pragmatic, 4, 47–50; *also see* justification, pragmatic
realism, 92; consistent with social-historical epistemology, 2, 51, 60, 64, 72–5, 87n7; empirical (Kant), 59; epistemological, 4, 59, 64, 71, 72–5, *defined*, 2, 53; internal (Putnam), 71, 92; naive, 58; pragmatic 73, 81n13, 87n7, 88, 114–5n20, *also see* realism, consistent with social-historical epistemology; *sans phrase*, transcendental argument for (Hegel), 65–71, 98; vs. historicist relativism, 2, 3, 72, 88, 102, 103, 107, 112–3, cf. 90
Realphilosophie (Hegel), 54
reason, 'in' nature, 53; vs. tradition, 77–9, 89–91; *also see* judgment, mature; rationality
Reason (*PhdG*), 63, 76
recognition, mutual, 60–2; thesis of, *defined*, 61
reductionism, of physical objects to sense data, 84, 85, 87–8, cf. 86n6
reference, descriptions theory of, 75–6; *defined*, 75
reflection, philosophical, 3–4, 69; transcendental (Kant), 11, 12, 69; *also see* judgment, reflective
reflective equilibrium, 49, 101
Refutation of Idealism (Kant), 59–60, 62, 65
regress argument, 9, 38, 45, 48, 50
relations, internal and external, 115n21
relativism, 48–9, 74; historicist, 2, 72, 88, 88n10, 98n6, 101, 103, cf. 89–91
relevant alternatives, *see* justification, relevant alternatives

Religion (*PhdG*), 64, 64n16
rule-following, 81n12; *also see* justification, deductive model of

schema (Kant), *defined*, 68n19
scheme, conceptual, 41, 42, 51, 75, 75–6; corrigibility of, 54, 63–64, 98, 100–1; relativity of, 42, 74, 75–6, 96, 101, *also see* relativism, historicist
science, the hypothesis of (Peirce), 114n20
seeing, nonepistemic, 94
seeing that, 94, 94n3; *also see* knowledge, propositional form of
Self-Alienated Spirit (*PhdG*), 63
Self-Consciousness (*PhdG*), 59, 62, 76
self-criticism, 7, 9, 12, 39, 40, 45, 49; constructive, 36, 45, 47, 40, 54, 90, 96, 100; *also see* consciousness, self-critical structure of; critique, internal
self-evidence, insufficiency of, 11, 28n17, 32, 38
self-knowledge, *see* self-understanding
Self-sufficiency and Non-Selfsufficiency of Self-Consciousness (*PhdG*), 59, 60
self-understanding, 32, 33–5, 37, 51, 54
semantic ascent, *defined*, 74; *also see* speech, modes of
sensation, 42–3, 45, 54, 55, 58, 65, 68–71, 78, 83, 83n2, 85–7, 88, 94, 94n3, 97, cf. 100, 100n9; *also see* concept-empiricism, experience, sense data
sense data, 54, 103; logical constructions of, 84, 85, 87n6
Sense Certainty (*PhdG*), 45, 58, 82, 84, 93
sensing strictly speaking (Descartes), 78

skepticism, five modes of (Agrippa), 9, 32, 45, 48, 50; Pyrrhonian, 2, 9, 36; responding to, 57; *also see* regress argument, question-begging
skills, 79, 80, 97, 104–6, 107, 109, 114; *also see* judgment, mature
sociology of knowledge, *see* knowledge, sociology of
sortals, *see* classification
source of information, *see* information, source
space, 59, conception of, *see* conceptions, pure a priori
speech, modes of, formal vs. material, 74; *defined,* 74n3
spirit, 54
Spirit (*PhdG*), 63–4
Spirit, Immediate (*PhdG*), *defined,* 31n6
spontaneity (of judgment), 79–80; *also see* autonomy
Strong Programme (sociology of knowledge), 107n10, cf. 112n16
subject, plural, 113–4; *defined,* 113
sublation, *see Aufhebung*
System of Philosophical Science (Hegel), 55

ta phainòmena (Aristotle), 7
The Moral World View (*PhdG*), 64
The Truth of Self-Certainty (*PhdG*), 59, 96

things, as unsensed causes of sensory experience, 54; in themselves (Kant), 59; *also see* particulars
throwing ball, 105–6
tradition, *see* norms, conventional
tradition vs. reason, *see* reason
traditionalism, 77, *also see* norms, conventional
training, *see* education
transcendental chaos, *see* chaos, transcendental
Treatise of Human Nature (Hume), 1, 84n3
True Spirit (*PhdG*), 63
truth, analysis of, correspondence, 51, 71, 73; condition, 46; criteria of, 40–4, 46, 49–50, 51, 73, 98, cf. 75, 81, *also see* justification, criteria of; minimalism about, 71; values, assignment of (Quine), 77n7, 103n2

Unhappy Consciousness (*PhdG*), 61

Vienna Circle, 83; *also see* empiricism, logical

wax, 87n7
Weltanschauung, 100, 101, 102
window, opening, 106
wisdom, 34; *also see* self-knowledge, self-understanding